CONTENTS

PART ONE:
The Generations
Silent Generation
Baby Boomers
Generation X
Millennials
Generations Y, Z… and iGen
Part TWO:
Millennial Myths
MYTH 1: Millennials Are Entitled
MYTH 2: Millennials Disrespect Authority
MYTH 3: Millennials are Lazy
MYTH 4: Millennials are Disloyal and Non-committal
MYTH 5: Millennials are Anti-Social
MYTH 6: Millennials Only Work at Trendy Companies
MYTH 7: Millennials are In an Exclusive Relationship with Technology
Conclusion

PART ONE:

THE GENERATIONS

The Generations

There I was standing in front of 50 realtors. iPhones had just come out, The Facebook was now just Facebook, Twitter was all the buzz and Burger Prince had officially changed its name to Burger King.

Okay, that last one wasn't true.

This was one of my first big speaking gigs and it dated all the way back to when I was still in high school. By this point I had launched my first company, a marketing firm. The firm quickly grew to a multinational marketing agency focusing on non-profits. To this day, I am not entirely sure if I was hired to speak because of my marketing agency or if they wanted me because I was a wide-eyed, clueless Millennial that had a Facebook Page and Twitter account that had gained nominal traction. Presumably, it was the latter.

These realtors had a problem. Millennials were not buying houses. Instead, after receiving a fancy degree from a prestigious university, they would sulk back home to the comforts of mom and dad's basement.

Mortgages, to the average Millennial, seemed impossible to obtain because of these self-employed couch surfers being their own boss. The banks viewed this as having no financial stability. These colleges grads would rather work on the gig-economy while taking advantage of newly minted laws that allowed them to stay on mommy and daddy's health insurance until the ripe age of twenty-six.

Don't even get me started on the idea of start-ups. For many, "launching a start-up," simply meant, "I'm unemployed but I'm working on the world's next greatest idea that will make me an overnight billionaire, just you wait." That said, not all start-ups were a smoke screen. In fact, as we will discuss later in the book, on more than one occasion, the Boomers taunted me about my early-stage ventures while the Gen X-ers rolled their eyes.

Fast forward to 2018. All Millennials officially were legal adults. That means every Millennial walking the planet can get married, vote, play the lottery, smoke and even get jury duty. Oh, the joys of adulting. Why is this important? Because, the Millennial generation is the largest generational cohort to walk the face of the planet.

With 75 million strong, individuals born between the early 1980s to 2000 are changing the way businesses are run, the way we communicate and the way we have to manage teams.

Not only do we have to learn how to effectively market to Millennials to continue to obtain new business, we must also learn how to manage Millennials. We are starting to see Millennials take over the workforce.

Simultaneously, the previous generations, predominantly led by the Baby Boomers, are leaving the workforce. This new era has created a litany of challenges for those in leadership. Managers are left scratching their heads, trying to figure out what in the world did society infuse into the brains of Millennials. Organizations are frustrated and these poor kids seemingly have no idea how to put in a real day's worth of work.

In order to understand Millennials, we need to look at the generations that have come before them. The reality is, history repeats itself. The best way to predict the future is to learn from the past. Let's go through United States' history and look at the different generations.

The actual years in which Millennials were born is widely debated. Some argue that Millennials are individuals that were born between 1980 and 2000. Others are firm on saying the last Millennial was born in 1994 and everyone after that is post-millennial or Generation Z. Still, others claim Generation Z as a part of the latter half of the Millennial cohort and reserve the term iGen (Generation I) for those born after 2000. While changing the parameter of a birth year does in fact impact some generalizations made about a group, for the purpose of this text, we will focus on Millennials being everyone born in the 1980s and 1990s.

At the end of reading this book, it is not my intention that you can concretely know someone's birth year by weird personality quirks or attitudes towards authority. Instead, the purpose is to give you a framework by which you can not only understand Millennials, but also understand both past and future generations. My hope is you will feel thoroughly equipped to market to, manage and motivate Millennials and all generations after reading.

One of the most fulfilling elements of speaking and doing workshops on the Millennial generation is when a Gen X or Boomer comes up to me afterwards thanking me. They do not thank me for helping them at work or become a better leader. Instead, they thank me for helping them better understand their own generation and how that intersects with Millennials. Nearly every time I present, *Cracking the Millennial Code*, a mother in her mid-to-late 50s will come up to me saying she now understands her children better than ever before.

Now, this is not an end all, be all. There is no magic formula. If you are hoping that this book will fix Millennials or give you the secret code to reprogram their brains to function more like a work drone, then you will get to the end and be disappointed. However, if you are willing to go into this open minded and realized that Millennials are likely only a fraction of your organizational challenges, you will likely walk away with new insights on how to best motivate and manage Millennials.

Let me be the first to admit, I am not a history expert. In fact, my academic track record in history was less than stellar. But, we cannot know where we are going unless we stop to understand where we have come from.

Stepping through the history of the generations may not make sense at first. Especially if the events happened far outside of your lifetime. As we get closer to your childhood and start talking about the events that you remember, it will likely all start to click. My hope is that you will be able to clearly see how one generation influenced the next, influenced the next, and influenced...Millennials.

Buckle up as we step back into the United States to the early 1900s and begin laying the foundation for everything you need to be equipped with to work with Millennials.

Silent Generation

Born between 1900-1945

The turn of the twentieth century was a new era for the United States of America. Barely one hundred twenty-five years old, the country was quickly rising to be the superpower that it is today.

In fact, the first five years of the twentieth century laid the foundation for innovation and implemented pillars of American culture. The first permanent motion picture theater, Tally's Electric Theater opened in Los Angeles in 1902. A year later, *The Great Train Robbery*, a twelve-minute long Western film, debuted. This advancement accelerated the growth of the film industry.

Earlier that same year, the United States held the first-ever World Series between the Pittsburgh Pirates and the Boston Americans (now known as the Red Sox). Boston won five of the eight games played, dubbing them the champion.

Still in 1903, both the Ford Motor Company and Harley-Davidson Motor Company were founded in the Midwest. Down on the east coast, more innovation was rapidly unfolding as the Wright brothers made their first powered flight in the *Wright Flyer.*

The Silent Generation, also known as the Traditionalists — is actually one of the longest spanning generational cohorts in America. While most generations are confined to a two-decade span or less, many historians argue the Silent Generation covers 45-years. While most agree that this group spans from 1900-1945, we are going to focus on the last two decades of this generation. Today, individuals in this cohort are seventy-five years old and older.

Members of the Silent Generation were born into a world where their parents rarely left the comforts of their local community. For their parents, transportation was limited, finances were tighter and small businesses thrived. However, as we will see, this Silent Generation entered the picture and experienced a whole new take on the world.

This generation is the first-ever generation to not know life without cars and even without air travel. The members of this generation undoubtedly have had the most tumultuous journey.

Historical Events

There are several key elements that shaped the culture and attitudes of the Silent Generation. Looking at the historical events that this generation faced during its formative years, it is undeniable that the Silent Generation grew up in some of the most trying times in all America's history.

Many of these individuals were born by parents who had tasted the roaring 20s — a sumptuously rich era. Think *The Great Gatsby*. Wealth was overflowing, new luxuries were brimming, alcohol was still legal (for the first time) and parties were lavish.

The extravagant celebrations of fortune were abruptly halted in 1929 by the infamous Wall Street Crash. The crash slid the economy right into the Great Depression. The bountiful years followed by pure depravity sent the country into chaos and misery. Crime increased. Jobs thinned. Money went missing.

The Depression lasted until 1939. During the Great Depression, food and jobs were difficult to come by. Many families lived on mere scraps or on food provided by the government, if they were lucky.

In 1936, President Roosevelt enacted The New Deal, which was a series of programs, public work projects, financial reforms and regulations as a response to The Great Depression. It was a proposition designed to get America back on its feet again and regain its prestigious superpower title.

As if the economic swings were not enough, the Silent Generation grew up during World War II (1939-1945). Though some were alive for World War I, they likely would not have remembered it as there were young children. What is vivid in the minds of this generation is early Sunday morning, on December 7, 1941 when President Roosevelt soberly announced the attack on Pearl Harbor.

The attack was just the start of yet another period of extreme uncertainty. Following the attack, rations were placed on food, gas and clothing. Though culturally, at the time, it was not overly common for women to work outside of the homes, the war changed things. Many women began working as electricians or welders to build materials needed for the war while their husbands fought overseas. Some members of the Silent Generation were of age to go overseas and fight for the first time. They were no longer kids. The younger subset of this generation saw brothers and fathers getting shipped across the Atlantic to fight for our freedoms. They would say their farewells knowing full well their return was no guarantee.

Stories of the roaring twenties seemed as mere fairy tales to members of the Silent Generation. The Great Depression and rations cut deep into their perception of money and material things. However, just as quick as World War II started in 1939, it ended in 1945 following the catastrophic bombings of Hiroshima and Nagasaki.

After World War II, the public perception of corporations rebounded. Trust in these corporate giants grew deeper for years to come. Though, peace in America did not even last five whole years.

In 1950, young American farmers joined the military as the country entered the Korean War. Yet again, the Silent Generation watched the country step back into turmoil. Though the Korean War ended in 1953, many Americans blamed President Truman and his administration for a lack of military preparedness. From that point forward, much of government funding went toward military equipment.

The constant barrage of hope and poverty, peace and war took a staggering toll on the Silent Generation. That impact was felt far beyond their generation and still lingers to this day. Not only was this generation accustomed to a rocky political climate, they were constantly being surprised by unprecedented innovations.

The Soviet Union launched Sputnik 1 in 1957 and sparked the Space Age. This was hot on the tail of the commercialization of the automobile and public air travel. Though America had accomplished many magnificent innovations in travel, Sputnik was yet another blow to the culture showing that Russia too had great potential. America fiercely competed with the Soviet Union to make advances in rocketry, science and computers.

Attitudes Towards Work and Finances

Ultimately, the Silent Generation was trying to figure out what it meant to live in a world that was unstable. Members of the Silent Generation saw what it meant to live frugally and in a time of uncertainty immediately followed by times of prosperity. However, the prosperity did not necessarily shape their mindset.

The Silent Generation was just trying to figure out how to maintain a normal life. They longed for stability. Many saw all of their parents' wealth get lost in the banking crisis. That was immediately followed by this generation witnessing their parents working exceptionally hard for every penny. In turn, the uncertainty and the hard-working condition caused the Silent Generation, as a whole, to develop a compulsion to be extremely frugal.

As a result, the Silent Generation was a firm believer in paying their dues in their respective workplaces. The generation as a whole was characterized by a strong desire of wanting to do whatever it took to make sure that they got all of their work done. Generally, this generation was committed to the organizations and companies they worked for and often developed great trust in their employers. Those employers were typically larger corporations. This generation wanted a shift from their parents' unstable and arduous manual labor. During the war, parents of the Silent Generation, usually their mothers, were the ones sewing uniforms. On the home front, these women would be working with scalding metal to help build ammunition and artillery.

The Silent Generation was witness to these very difficult work environments, but they believed in paying their dues. Why? Because they wanted to be loyal to their country. They saw the United States stand victorious time and time again, though it was not easy. It cost millions of lives. If a member of the Silent Generation was not yet old enough to fight in the war, they more than likely saw their fathers and brothers fight overseas and their mothers work hard to make sure the men had what they needed to win the war. As a result, the Silent Generation, though scarred by the turbulence of war, became loyal to family and country. To this day, a loyal attitude is ingrained into the way in which they work. That said, the majority of this cohort is retired.

They have a loyalty to "the man." This attitude permeated their generation. The members of the Silent Generation became company people and they would never, ever question authority or rank. In fact, this complacency in the workplace is one of the reasons they were assigned the title "Silent Generation." Many members of the generational cohort were going to go to work and keep their heads down. More often than not, they would do whatever they needed to do to prove their loyalty.

The Silent Generation is characterized for their persistence in adhering to the rules, dedication to work, family, country, and their respect for authority. For this generation, career development was not an option. They were taught to keep their nose to the grindstone and work hard, but only a few got to move up within an organization.

As they started to earn money, this generation firmly believed in putting their money away. Many would literally stash their cash under their mattress because of a strong distrust for banks. This skepticism is one of many ripple effects that lingered after The Great Depression. Members of the Silent Generation typically pay only in cash. They are frugal. Saving tin foil and washing out resealable plastic bags was a part of their life. While many in this cohort went on to have successful careers and pensions that more than provided for them financially, the generation always was concerned with security. So, they saved as much as possible. Money was their livelihood. But more than that, money was their rock and cornerstone.

Members of the Silent Generation have a unique view on money. Money is better kept hidden in a safe rather than spent. So, while most members of this generation have a generous nest egg, they will likely not touch it in their lifetime. Even with hundreds of thousands in savings for their retirement, they will be concerned that they will go poor. Chances are, they fully own their house and their car and have no debt. Many never had a credit card. This extreme frugality and fear of losing money, as we will soon see, wreaked havoc on the Baby Boomers' perception of money. But let's not get ahead of ourselves.

Home Life

The individuals in the Silent Generation were raised by parents that had just survived the Great Depression. They experienced hard times while growing up and reached prosperity as adults. Families during this generation were traditional, nuclear families — two parents, a man and a woman, married to each other. As children, most never knew what a broken home looked like. Divorce was never an option.

This idealistic family life shaped this generation. It evoked a dedicated sense of loyalty and an understanding of the family unit. The Silent Generation experienced a flurry of emotions and ups and downs. Because of their checkered pasts — from war heroes to mega-celebrities — these individuals have many attributes in common.

When being interacted with, even to this day, some things hold true. Most Silent Generation members demand respect. It is ingrained. They will give respect but also expect respect in return. Disrespect, especially towards authority, is not an option. They are loyal to their country. The wars taught them that. They are loyal to their company. The Great Depression taught them that. They are loyal to their family. Divorce was not an option.

Education

For children of the Silent Generation, education was a dream. One-room schoolhouses were normal. Most people, particularly women, never actually got an education past the sixth grade. This is a characteristic of many in this generation, especially those born earlier. For individuals born in the thirties and forties, education became more widely available, though still not totally accessible by everyone.

The members of the Silent Generation that were fortunate to attend both elementary and secondary school during the thirties and forties were often the teachers and administrators of the 1950s through the 1990s. It is a clear depiction of a prior generation trying to care for the next generation by providing for others what they did not have for themselves. This theme repeats itself time and time again--sometimes for the good. Other times, to the detriment of the next generational cohort. The more educated members of the Silent Generation set the tone for academics across the country. The influence and precedent spread well into the seventies and eighties.

Cultural Motivators

The Silent Generation felt it was dangerous to speak out. Unlike nearly every other generation we will look at, the Silent Generation rarely would advocate for causes. As a whole, many members felt they were most effective if they kept their head down, held a family together and earned money for safety and security. This is not a generation that took to the streets or fought against the government. They would do what their bosses would tell them to do and go where their country would send them to fight. Their name, the

"Silent Generation" stems from their reputation of complacency. Many members of the Silent Generation fought in the Korean War (1950-1953).

As part of the war, American troops entered the war on South Korea's behalf. Nearly two million Americans served in Korea during the war and more than thirty-six thousand Americans died there. Sadly, these efforts are often referred to as "the forgotten war" and a proper tribute was not paid to those soldiers until 1991.

Interestingly enough, Conscription, better colloquially known as "the draft," had been invoked in numerous wars throughout America's history. While there was always some level of protest, during the Korean War, there was a much more passive take on the draft. Again, this proves the generation's loyalty towards country and passiveness in tribulation. In a fascinating survey recorded by Gallup in February of 1953, 70 percent of Americans felt the system in place for Selected Services and the draft were fair. In the same survey, qualified men that could have served were questioned. Astonishingly, 64 percent of that cohort also agreed that the government was fair.

A decade earlier, during World War II, many groups were rising up to protest the draft. While some new legislation was implemented, the impact remained almost identical. Yet, you can see the stark contrast in attitudes towards the government even across a decade.

Innovation

It is probably no surprise that technology, as we view it today, was not a large part of this generation. However, the foundation and groundwork for much of our modern-day innovation actually started with the Silent Generation.

Communication and transportation were among the most novel advancements of the time. The United States became a bit smaller. Media started to have an influence on the Silent Generation, knitting the country together with news spreading more quickly. After World War I, many households started purchasing radios. By World War II, radios became a staple in the home. Many Silent Generation members heard music aired live for the first time in their childhood. Top 40 stations became popular. By the end of the Korean War, televisions also started to become a mainstay in homes. That said, broadcasting was limited to only a few channels, often referred to as the "Big Four." They are all still around today--ABC, NBC, CBS and Fox. The programming back in the 1950s was not quite what we know it to be today. There were shorter newscasts that ran nowhere close to 24/7/365. You would dial into a given channel at a preset time to catch the news. When the news was syndication had ended, you would turn off your TV and get back to the family.

This generation also saw the invention of the rotary-dial telephone, which first appeared in 1892 in Indiana. However, it wasn't until 1919 that national service for rotary phones truly began. This invention sparked a golden age for communication. Before rotary phones, calls would go through a commercial telephone exchange, which required a human operator to connect calls using patch cables. In war times, some people would have to wait two hours to be connected with loved ones. The rotary-dial telephone cut out the middleman and made communication much easier.

For the first time, the world was being connected in real time. Transportation also had a huge role. Most individuals in the Silent Generation do not remember life without cars. That said, cars were for the wealthy. It was not until the 1950s that it became normal for many families to have a car. Cars were unreliable and often broke down. They were noisy and reeked of the gas that they were burning through.

As a result of the increase in motor vehicles, domestic travel increased. Roadside diners and motels began popping up as families would travel to see loved ones in other states. The Interstate Highway Act of 1956 accelerated the growth of cars and ease of transport. While airplanes existed at the time, it was not a common mode of travel. It was reserved for the most wealthy. It would not be until individuals in the Silent Generation were well into adulthood that they would take their first flight.

The United States infrastructure from electricity to roads to communication to airports started to boom during the Silent Generation's formative years. The Hoover Dam — built from 1931-1936 — was an impressive introduction to technology the country had never seen before. The job required more than 5,000 construction workers, and they were going to build a dam that generated hydroelectric power... all in a remote desert region of the country. At the time, it was the highest dam in the world, and it took some innovative engineering to cool and set the large amounts of concrete. During that same time, the Golden Gate Bridge was constructed. Not only were these major feats of engineering, they symbolized the country's growth and increasing expansion out West.

The Recap

The Silent Generation grew up in a time of wealth and poverty, peace and wars. Their biggest desire was to keep everything status quo. They longed for financial stability, so they were loyal to their companies. This generation wanted a peaceful homelife that stayed together, so they believed strongly in the power of a traditional nuclear family. Members of this generation saw the potential in the future of the United States with its innovation and expansion, so they silently were loyal to their country.

To this day, respect and loyalty are key to this generation's happiness and success. While most members of the Silent Generation have retired from their careers, they still believe in mutual and shared respect to everyone they work with. More than other generations, the Silent Generation values age and sees a clear pecking order based on the number. They believe that someone who has paid their dues by putting in the time deserves to be rewarded. It is not solely based on quality of work as much as character and mutual trust.

Baby Boomers

Born between 1946-1964

World War II ended six years and one day after it began, on September 2, 1945. The troops finally started their journey home. Though air travel existed and transatlantic flights blossomed as a result of the war, troops mainly returned home via ship. That means, after fighting a brutal war, these soldiers would transverse back across the Atlantic via boat. The voyage could take weeks.

By the time the soldiers landed back stateside, it was well into autumn. The seasons had changed. The weather, brisk. Central heating had not quite entered the picture, so these soldiers were reunited with their wives in a chilly home. When it gets cold, people cuddle. And in 1945, when people cuddled...we got the Baby Boomers.

All of the sudden, there was a massive population spike in the three-to-four years following World War II. For almost an entire decade following World War II, babies were born at a rate of four million per year in the United States. To put it into perspective, that is approximately double the rate of births both in generations before and after.

During the birth years of the Silent Generation, there was a slight decline in new babies immediately following The Great Depression and again, a more noticeable decline during World War II. But have no fear, the Silent Generation wasted no time making up for the slight slowdown as they began rapidly repopulating the earth.

Enter the Baby Boomers. Boomers were the largest generational cohort ever. Well, until the Millennials came onto the scene. The Boomers came in with a bang. In fact, to this day, there has never been consecutive years with exponentially increased birth rates recorded.

The rapid birth rate remained well-above average for nearly a decade. However, the steep incline dropped dramatically in the sixties. The sharp decline is one of the only reasons the Millennial generation ended up surpassing the size of the Baby Boomer cohort. The other fact is simply the law of exponential growth. Most historians agree that the Boomer generation spans individuals born from 1946-1964.

The parents of this new generation had seen a tremendous amount of history being written as we saw in the previous chapter. They fought in wars, saw the impact of the wars, worked in sweatshops, were not necessarily educated and they desperately had to figure out what it meant to be parents. When loved ones came back from the war, there was little time to rekindle a relationship before little junior was on the way. Many Silent Generation parents, with Boomer children, did not know how to parent well. They were more concerned about keeping peace in the family. Remember, the Silent Generation, as a whole, was loyal to their companies, their country, and they really wanted to be loyal to their kids. We will see in a moment how this panned out.

The mindset and experiences of the Silent Generation had a staggering impact on Boomers. At the time of this book, most of the members of the Baby Boomer generation are upper-middle-aged and are the most seasoned workers in the workforce. Most Boomers sit in leadership roles and have replaced their predecessors, the Silent Generation.

Historical Events

Baby Boomers were born at a unique time. They never saw the United States go to war. That is an important anecdote. As far as most Boomers can remember, America had always been in the middle of a war.

Boomers, as a whole, were used to the country being in a state of constant conflict. The conflict between the US and the Soviet Union that started the Cold War began in 1946 and didn't de-escalate until 1989. That turmoil spans the majority of Baby Boomers' formative years.

Life in America became a time of nuclear preparedness. Schools and businesses practiced "duck-and-cover" drills while homeowners built nuclear fallout shelters. Mass paranoia about a possible Soviet invasion became a way of life.

Not only was the arms race on the forefront of news cycles, the Vietnam War was also in full swing from 1954-1975. The Vietnam War arguably had a much more profound impact on the Boomers' perception of the United States as well as their entire outlook on life.

At the time, the voting age was twenty-one. During the war, the idea that eighteen-year-old men could be drafted without having the privilege to vote caused great angst. Pressure mounted for legislators to lower the voting age across the country. Eventually, the twenty-sixth Amendment was passed and ratified in 1971. However, many men had already been sent overseas without the right to vote. Some losing their life. This political faux pas began to foster an anti-government view that many Baby Boomers adopted.

Despite the fact that Baby Boomers were born into a period where the United States was at war, many were numb to the international conflict. They never saw the shock and momentum of going to war. This generation was born into a state of global unrest.

Cultural Motivators

Naturally, we all want to be in control. It is human nature. It provides us a sense of security. As the Baby Boomers witnessed conflict happening on foreign soil, they wanted to do something. They wanted to take control. However, growing up as young adolescents into early adulthood, there was little they could do to impact change in the struggle overseas. As a result, the Boomers are one of the first documented generation to take a stance. Though their stance was focused internally saying, "Something is broken and I need to fix it." Part of this drive stems from the freedom and autonomy they received from their parents as children.

Since they realized they could not fix battles thousands of miles away across the ocean, they turned inward to remedy what was within grasp. Enter Martin Luther King, Jr. Though a member of the Silent Generation (born in 1929) he was the domestic hero the country needed. His cause for civil rights revolutionized the Boomer generation.

In 1955, he led the first non-violent demonstration of contemporary times in the United States. It lasted 382 days. King stood for fairness and equality-- something that the Boomers deeply desired. That is not to say the Boomers all wanted or even to this day want equal rights across ethnicities and genders. However, the notion of fighting for a cause and having the freedom to express oneself is what the Boomers related to most – regardless of their personal feelings towards racial reconciliation and equality.

At the end of 1956, the United States Supreme Court declared that segregation laws, specifically related to seating on buses, were unconstitutional. Between 1957 and 1968, King spoke more than twenty-five hundred times, led protests and marches around the country, and was arrested upwards of twenty times. He was a leader and a rebel that spoke his mind. He knew he could not fix the world, but he challenged inequality at home in the United States. Again, tackling issues on the home front related well with Boomers. The movement was tangible. Stirring change on US soil empowered the Boomers to not feel utterly hopeless about being able to influence change overseas.

Sadly, not all Baby Boomers were advocates of racial equality. Some were getting bored of that fight--others had no interest. One thing most Boomers have in common is the fact that they loved to rebel against convention-- beginning with their conservative parents. This generation was filled with revolutionists. Baby Boomers questioned everything. With media broadcasting becoming more advanced, more people became more aware of the issues of the world. They were not content with the status quo.

The end of the Vietnam War brought mounting mistrust amongst the public, specifically in regard to government officials. Americans of this generation had little trust in its leaders. These feelings were further solidified when Richard Nixon's presidency ended in 1974 after the Watergate Scandal of 1972.

Boomers were not merely political and civil activists. Other major cultural shifts began unfolding. In 1960, the first oral contraceptive, Enovid, was approved by the US Food and Drug Administration. The pharmaceutical breakthrough opened the curtain on the Sexual Revolution. A new era dawned where young adults (the Boomers by this time) felt free to explore their sexuality. Sex was no longer a curse word but instead was a word used as an act of self-expression. For the first time, women were no longer viewed solely as mothers and home keepers. They had sexual desires and independent free spirits--just like men. This defied the Silent Generation's moral standards.

Historians say the movement primarily took place between the sixties and the eighties in the United States. But, as we will read in the coming pages, the revolution lives on. Eventually, it spread around the world. As we will discover in a moment, the Sexual Revolution is a leading factor to the capitulation of the traditional American family.

Around the same time, music became readily accessible. In the summer of 1969, the original Woodstock Festival brought together half a million people in a celebration of peace, music and love. These were the core values of the generation. The festival took place on a dairy farm in Bethel, New York, and featured thirty-two music acts over the course of four days. Crowds heard music from Jimi Hendrix, the Grateful Dead, Janis Joplin and many more culturally provocative artists.

Woodstock is known as one of the greatest happenings of all time and perhaps the most pivotal moment in musical history. During this time, music started to have a heavy influence on culture. Throughout the mid-century years, there was a form of self-expression that had never been seen before in America.

It is important to note that music has not always been accessible like it is today. A lot of people forget that. Even Boomers who grew up during this era tend to forget that music was not something that you could always just pop your headphones in and listen to whenever you wanted. Yes, there were radio stations and record stores. But music was not as prevalent as it is today.

The Boomers grew up to be the radicals of the seventies and the yuppies of the eighties. They were filled with radical idealism as they refused to be like their parents who were always at war. Because of this, they started trying to bring peace back to the United States.

Remember, the Silent Generation stayed silent and just took life as it came. They were not ones to speak up. The Boomer generation was different. They knew that something was broken so they were much more outspoken. They longed for change.

Attitudes Towards Work and Finances

For Baby Boomers, Christmas gifts were limited to a gift or two per child. Their parents were often frugal and had limited money to spend due to the quantity of children they had post-war. Boomers grew to resent the stingy nature of their parents. Forget reusing wrapping paper. Baby Boomers wanted to live a much more lavish and free life – liberated from the clutches of money.

For the first time, the American Dream moved away from the original notion of an immigrant's desire to gain citizenship in the United States. It took on a new meaning: one with a picturesque white picket fence around a single-family home, two point two kids and a golden retriever. Though Boomers were not necessarily victims of poverty growing up, many felt robbed of life's luxuries due to their parents' tight purse strings. As children, the American Dream was promised to the Boomers. The idea that they could be whoever they wanted to be and have whatever they wanted to have when they grew up was taught to them from childhood. So, they worked hard to attain it. This led to a very greedy and materialistic generation.

Many Baby Boomers desired to work hard. In fact, they worked so hard, the idea of the sixty-hour work week was born. Not only did this generation birth this workplace culture, they are the chief enforcers of the concept – even to this day. Boomers were — and still are — loyal to their work. Sucking up to the boss became the norm. Climbing the corporate ladder was the goal. This was a major cultural shift that still influences companies to this day. Most executive leadership roles are now filled by Boomers, so this idea of long working hours is still very much present.

While the Silent Generation put heavy emphasis on quality, the Baby Boomers focused on quantity. Boomers often think, "If I work until 6:30pm and my boss leaves before me, I've done a good job." To a Boomer, it is more important to look busy and productive to prove loyalty to their employer than it is to produce quality work. Whereas the Silent Generation's main identity is wrapped up in family, a Boomer's is often wrapped up in their title and their work. Again, these are generalizations. There are exceptions to every rule.

Boomers are often hesitant to take time off because they feared losing their position on the corporate team. As a result, there is a clear imbalance between work and family that starts to form.

If you were to ask a member of the Silent Generation, "Tell me about yourself." They would likely talk about their family, where they are from and then maybe what they do. If you were to ask the same question to a Baby Boomer, chances are, they would rattle off their title and company. They may or may not mention their family or where they are from.

One major difference from the older Baby Boomers to the younger ones is the fact that the older Baby Boomers started to mentor the younger Boomers and even Gen X-ers. For the first time, we see a previous generation assuming an almost parental role in the workplace. However, this was not always the case in their home.

As a whole, Boomers were and are more willing to bring someone along as an apprentice and watch them grow through the ranks — this is unlike many other generational cohorts. Despite their helpfulness to their younger co-workers, Boomers wanted to be the stars. This stardom mindset that did not before exist. If you think about it, Boomers were the first generation to experience a thriving pop-culture. From the rise of movie theaters to television shows, musical acts to radio dramas, Boomers were the first to be exposed, almost daily, to the concept of celebrities.

While few go onto be Hollywood stars, many Boomers still wanted to make a name for themselves. Meaning, they started to want to have elaborate corporate titles, fancy cars, and mortgages they could barely afford. The generation took a step back in history towards an era more similar to the roaring twenties.

The Baby Boomers were more likely to go into debt than other generations past. Money was a status symbol. Credit cards were becoming popular and commonplace for the first time. With credit and loans more accessible, they were more likely to buy a bigger house and a nicer car. The Baby Boomers spent money like crazy, mostly because they could. Their feeling towards money was, "Spend now, worry later."

By 1960, seventy-five percent of this country owned a car. As Boomers came of driving age, there was a good chance their family had a car that they would learn to drive. Yet again, this is a major societal milestone that the Boomers were able to experience first. For the first time, it was now considered normal for houses to be built with two-car garages. All of these cultural shifts began unfolding primarily because this generation was accumulating more money than ever before. In addition to the sixty-hour work week, you had many households that had two working adults. Not only were wages on the rise, but that pay increase was now multiplied times two. At this rate, American households had an exponential increase in expendable income.

Education

Education for the Baby Boomers was no longer something that happened in a one-room schoolhouse. It was no longer a pipe dream for women. Sixth grade now marked the halfway point, not a finish line. By this time, almost everyone had graduated from high school — it was rare for someone not to graduate high school. College was becoming something that was most certainly not required by prospective employers, but definitely encouraged. Going to a trade school or something similar was definitely noble.

Boomers started to see education as a part of what they needed to do. For the first time, going to college became a normal part of all these people's lives. While the popularity of attending college was on the rise, it was quite uncommon for both people in a marriage to have gone to college. During this time, women's educational achievement stagnated. For many school age women of the time, graduating high school was enough. In the fifties, there was a growing tendency for women to consider housework as an expression of their femininity.

Home Life

The sitcom, *Leave it to Beaver* portrayed the cheerful, all-American family throughout the 1950s. The show follows a family of four. The father, Ward, was the breadwinner. June, the wife and mother, maintained the home.

For many Boomers, this family-life scenario was a reality growing up. It was what media portrayed. This sitcom, along with others such as *The Andy Griffith Show*, were the first glimpses ever, into someone else's family life. However, as the Boomers became parents, the idealistic sitcom family-life rode off into the sunset.

In 1946, the infamous *Baby and Childcare* book by Dr. Benjamin Spock, hit the shelves. The book had an impact on the parenting of Boomers. Parents wanted peaceful homes. After all, the parents (Silent Generation) were tired of turmoil. The picturesque views of home aired on television. Plus, literature like Dr. Spock's book encouraged idea of parents befriending their children, the Boomers. Growing up in this environment, Boomers had more freedom than prior generations. The book, along with culture at the time, encouraged open communication and a less authoritarian approach to parenting. Mutual respect was huge. Children were to be respectful towards parents. Other than that, Boomers often grew up in a time where they had free reign. They could ride their bike to the corner store without supervision. Going over to a friend's house after school was assumed and parents questioned little. Perish the thought that a Silent Generation parent should question their adolescent, Boomer child when they arrived home late wreaking of alcohol. That would have stirred up conflict. It would have disrupted the peaceful, friendly home environment.

With all major cultural shifts, there are consequences. As a result of the laissez-faire parenting, the Boomer generation has been referred to as the "Me" generation. Unfortunately, this inward attitude is what led to the highest divorce rate in history, along with the highest rate for second marriages. The American Dream of equality and prosperity became more important than family life for many Boomers throughout their twenties, thirties and often into their forties.

The hard work prevented many Boomers from marrying young. On average, Boomers would get married two-to-three years later in life than their parents. In addition, they were having their first child almost five years later than their parents. Longer schooling, more dedication to work and improved birth control methods are all factors in contributing to these shifts.

Combine the longer work hours with the explosion of media and consider the picture. There were more channels on TV, modern-day styled sitcoms began, and evenings were spent in front of a screen. By 1960, eighty-seven percent of families had a television. All of this contributed to the self-centered tone of this generation, and the traditional structure of the American family began to break.

Innovation

In 1946, the microwave was invented by Percy Spencer. The first few models were large and expensive. If you wanted to nuke your food, you would have to fork out approximately $2,000. So, it wasn't until 1967 when an affordable, more modern-style microwave — called the "compact Radarange" — made it to the countertops in American homes. It took a few years to convince consumers that the low amount of radiation was safe and the government created legislation putting limits on radiation levels for the microwave and other inventions. With the rise of television consumption, TV tray dinners made their debut.

In 1970, ten percent of American households had a microwave. By 1975, one million microwaves were sold every year for around $500 each. Throughout the seventies, cookware companies started to produce lines of dishes specifically designed for microwave use. The microwave certainly made dinner preparation much easier, and families were able to reheat their food without using extra dishes or re-cooking entire meals.

As Boomers moved from childhood to adulthood, the quantity of microwavable dinners rivaled what it is today. When Boomers hit their stride in their career and were fighting for a corporate title, it was not uncommon to work late nights. The microwave was the perfect excuse not to be home for a warm family dinner. Leftovers could be sealed up, put in the refrigerator and heated up.

Sure, microwavable Hungry-Man dinners made a dent in the future of our country, but innovation in communication was also on the rise. The telephone became more than a rotary-dial. In 1963, President John F. Kennedy started a countdown to the opening of the World's Fair by keying "1964" on a touch-tone phone inside the Oval Office. That same year, push-button touch-tone phones made their debut to the general public. Though a seemingly insignificant innovation today, the touch-tone phone changed the form factor of telephones paving ways for new innovations and multiple phones throughout a home. Sales for the touch-tone phone picked up in the seventies and continued for decades to come.

One of the most significantly influential innovations was the personal computer. Though the personal computer looked far different than it does today, it was the Boomer generation that grew up in this season of innovation. In the late 1970s, Apple made its debut. Computers were no longer for geeks and hobbyists. Computers started to become a mainstay.

By the time many Boomers went off to college or entered their first job, they almost certainly had access to a computer or two. In fact, the later-born Boomers probably had their very own computer at their first professional job. The era of electric typewriters was phasing out and the age of word processing was walking on stage. Little did anyone know just how revolutionary the personal computer would be.

The Space Age was in full swing. Boomers were born into a world with their heads in the stars. Movies like *E.T.* were popular for Boomers as they entered their late teens and early twenties. Nearly all Boomers have some recollection of where they were on July 29, 1969. Crackling from fuzzy communication being beamed back to earth from the moon nearly a quarter of a million miles away, Neil Armstrong proclaimed, "That's one small step for man, one giant leap for mankind." And so it was, the landing of Apollo 11 on the moon was ingrained in the minds of Boomers. It unlocked potential. Boomers are the first generation to grow up thinking that the sky was no longer limit, that the universe was.

The moon landing was just one of many major milestones in space exploration. The first US satellite, Explorer 1, went into orbit on January 31, 1958. In 1961, Alan Shephard became the first American to fly into space. In 1962, John Glenn's historic flight made him the first American to orbit Earth.

The Recap

Baby Boomers took their parents' traditional ways and tossed them out the window. Career and the pursuit of money and materialistic wealth became a focal point. As children, Boomers were exposed to the possibility of what could be. Moving into their adolescent and young adult years, Boomers became activists. They were not content with the world as they knew it. Though they could not fix the wars overseas, they could attempt to fight inequality and lack of freedoms here in the United States. As a result, they focused on self-expression and outward proclamations of their new world views.

Entering their careers, Boomers had a cut-throat mentality. The corporate ladder to nowhere was the most important thing, front and center. The more money they could earn, the bigger house they could have. The bigger house came with a bigger garage in which they could store their fancy cars. To this day, Baby Boomers in the workplace demand dedication to a company. They expect long hours and personal sacrifice from their employees.

The self-focused, career-driven nature of the generation caused a slight delay in marriages and an even longer delay in children being born. Boomers are among the most likely to say something along the lines of, "When I was your age…" as if to inform a younger generation that they have it easier. Part of that is the Boomer's natural tendency to spin the spotlight back around on themselves and their achievements. It is the manifestation of the American Dream--these Boomers want you to know they came from humble beginnings, but now for you to see where they have come and what they have accomplished.

Generation X

Born between 1965-1980

Generation X, also referred to as Gen X-ers, were born into a very different world than their Boomer parents. They saw a different era. During this time, wars were ending, things were getting better, and America was solidifying itself as a world superpower. Gen X-ers were born into large homes with at least two cars and happy parents. Then, all of a sudden, the utopia would come crashing back down. America's stability once again started to bounce around as international events started unraveling.

Today, in 2019, Gen X-ers are in their late thirties to mid-fifties.

This generation grew up quickly, which is something important to note. Not only did they have more access to media, but where most psychologists and sociologists say that generations typically came of age around eighteen to twenty-years-old, they would argue that Gen X-ers came of age anywhere from thirteen to eighteen-years-old. By coming of age, these researchers simple are assessing an age at which an individual realizes and is frequently exposed to adult situations--no not an explicit movie scene. Instead, this is an indication of when an individual is aware of war and peace, human interactions, economic situations and the political landscape. This moment is marked by a time when the carefree nature and innocence of a child is lost to the harsh realities of the depravity of humanity. At the core, increased media presence and new modalities of communication are the primary reason.

Historical Events

In June of 1972, an investigation was initiated after a break-in to the Democratic National Committee headquarters in Washington, D.C. What seemed like a mere break-in led to a much larger investigation. In no time, it became clear the burglars were connected to President Nixon's reelection campaign. Alas, the Watergate Scandal.

The robbery was just the tip of the iceberg. As the investigation was underway, it shed light on a cacophony of elicit behaviors including the abuse of presidential power and deliberate obstruction of justice. The House Judiciary Committee voted to impeach Nixon for violating the United States Constitution. Nixon resigned shortly after.

At the time members of the Generation X cohort were children or not even born yet. However, due to the common practice of families leaving television sets on as well as the increase in availability of news and communication, many Gen-Xers have faint recollection of the scandal.

Fast forward two decades. For about half of Gen X-ers, the first time they were able to go to the polls and vote to elect a president was for the 1992 and 1996 elections. In 1992, President Bill Clinton beat out incumbent President George H.W. Bush. And in 1996, President Clinton was reelected. Just two years after taking office a second time, President Clinton issued his famous statement, "I did not have sexual relations with that woman…"

Starting with Watergate but being solidified by the Clinton-Lewinsky scandal, Gen X-ers largely distrust politicians. Beyond the nefarious behaviors of the country's leaders, many Gen X-ers recall other political and diplomatic friction. As children in the 1970s, members of Generation X witnessed the Energy Crisis. As the automobile industry was climbing, so was gasoline consumption.

While oil usage increased in the United States, domestic oil production was declining. This put an increasing dependency on imported oil. In 1973, the Organization of Arab Petroleum Exporting Countries put an embargo on oil. As a result, the price of oil went from three dollars per barrel to twelve dollars per barrel. At the date of this book's publication, oil is sitting around sixty dollars a barrel. However regardless of today's prices, a four times increase in the price of anything is significant.

Following the price spikes of oil and gas, America fell into a massive oil shortage. To conserve oil and energy, the government asked gas stations to close every Sunday and advised homeowners to skip hanging Christmas lights. The embargo was a huge blow to the automobile industry. Quickly, American manufacturers were outpaced by those in Japan who created smaller, more fuel-efficient models. Although the embargo was lifted in 1974, oil prices remained high and Americans saw the effects of the energy crisis for the following decade.

In the eighties and the early nineties, a large number of US companies announced major restructuring and downsizing, resulting in many layoffs. General Electric Chairman, Jack Welch, was popularizing the idea of layoffs as a sign of corporate competitiveness. Those being laid-off did not see it that way. Jobs were disappearing as companies moved their factories abroad. Young people who came of age during these layoffs grew up with an understanding that there was nothing they could do to resist a similar fate.

The end of the Cold War came in 1991, and the United States was seen as a rising world power, along with China. The era following the Cold War was dominated by globalization, enabled by the commercial internet and the popularity of mobile phones.

Of course, there was the scare of Y2K. As the year 2000 was approaching, Gen X-ers were just getting into their careers. Most of them were in their early twenties and they were excited to be out in the real world. Then rumors began unfolding as the end of the millennia neared. It was rumored that computers could not handle the year 2000 and they would fry.

Y2K or, the "Millennium bug" was a computer bug or a flaw that was said to have caused problems when understanding dates after December 31, 1999. Computer programmers in the sixties through the eighties only used two digits for the year, so 1999 was programmed into a computer as 99.

These programmers feared that computers may understand 00 as 1900 instead of 2000. Personal computers were one thing, but banks, centers of technology, power plants and airlines would all be affected if computers went back to January 1, 1900. Many computers were reprogrammed in preparation for the date change. Even those that were not updated accordingly functioned fine.

Home Life

With the Boomers working long hours and both parents holding down jobs, their kids, (Generation X) had to fend for themselves. And so, the era of latchkey kids began.

Latchkey kids are children that had dual working parents. These young school-aged children would come home after class and took care of themselves. They would walk themselves home, prepare their own after school snack and hang out around the neighborhood until early evening when mom and dad would final roll home from their corporate America job.

This is the first generation of children where it was commonplace not to have mom home after school. In fact, women were not only permitted to, but they were expected to work outside of the home. It was widely accepted and even encouraged that women should have careers of their own.

Gen X-ers were usually unwatched for hours at a time. Their hardworking parents (Baby Boomers) felt that working long-hours would allow them to better provide for their children. This was a result of the Boomer's parents, the Silent Generation, often working one job and being extremely frugal. Now we are really seeing the trickle-down impact.

As a result of being home and fending for themselves, members of Generation X are generally self-starters. They will look for things that need done and they will do it. Growing up being home alone, if they wanted something, they often had no one to rely on but themselves. This self-reliance and self-starting attitude is loved by many employers of Generation X.

Unfortunately, the parents of Generation X also had the highest divorce rate. Relationships often began in the workplace causing infidelity. Sometimes the purse busyness and exhaustion of both a husband and wife working sixty-hour-weeks and then coming home to their kids put entirely too much strain on a relationship. The marriages would snap. The divorce rate climbed.

The Boomer's traditionally self-centered nature often led to an increase in divorce as well. They wanted their needs to be met. Conflict was familiar to the Boomers with the constant wars they were exposed to. Coupled with the Sexual Revolution and focus on self-gratification, it is no surprise that the marriages crumbled. The previous generation's decision greatly impacted the growth in divided homes. Fractured homes were "normal" for Generation X. They did not know differently.

Not only were Gen X-ers often home alone, they knew what it was like to live in two homes. They lived with one parent during the week and moved in with the other parent on the weekend. This generation grew up in very unhealthy homes.

As a result of their splintered families, Generation X wanted to do things differently when they had children. Despite the broken homes, members of Generation X were often married by the age of twenty-five. The median age for marriage is only a fraction of a year older than the average age their parents were married. Further, most would have children within the first several years of being married.

Contrary to their parents, Generation X was not as focused on working long hours allowing them more time to date and start a family.

To reverse the cycle of divorce, Gen X-ers wanted to be home more with their families. The high divorce rate their parents had was not something they wanted to repeat. Sadly, because many did not have a good example of a healthy marriage, the cycle continued and divorce rates remains fairly steady.

The result of broken homes led to smaller families. Plus, many Baby Boomer parents did not want to spend their hard-earned cash on caring for a large family, so the averaged about two and a half children. There were almost two Baby Boomers for every one Gen X-er. This cohort was drastically smaller than both its predecessor (Boomers) and successor (Millennials).

Education

Many from the Generation X group excelled in school. They had to truly learn how to do their homework--mom and dad were not home to help. With a lack of access to computers in their grade school years, Gen X-ers had to work exceptionally hard on projects. They were often on their own. This self-reliance created a higher caliber work from many in the generation.

In 1965, President Lyndon B. Johnson signed the Elementary and Secondary Education Act, which was a call for congressional efforts to improve education opportunities in America.

For Gen X-ers college was starting to become expected. Instead of working longer hours when they made it to their careers, Generation X began relying a bit more on their degree and academic pedigree. Movies flourished during this generation. Growing up in the 1980s, you went and saw some of the greatest blockbusters of all time. You also could still go to Blockbuster, may it rest in peace.

Both the rise of collegiate education and popularity in cinema, movies like "Revenge of the Nerds" and "Animal House" were born. When a Gen X-er headed off to college, they typically would not have access to a personal computer. In class, they often used a notebook and pen for taking notes. Encyclopedias were still the prized possessions of libraries and were primarily used for researching topics. Libraries were the epicenter of research, study and homework. Professors were, for the first time, requiring computer-typed assignments and reports. So, many Gen X-ers would head to the computer lab and wait their turn to write up their final reports.

College tuition was approximately $10,000 annually. Many would start college but not all would finish. Some attrition was due to cost, others starting a family and still others pursuing a career without a bachelors. Approximately thirty-five percent of Gen X-ers in the United States have a bachelor's degrees.

Attitudes Towards Work and Finances

Generation X experienced first had the family impact of having no work-life balance. Some Gen X-ers were burned by the hectic schedules their parents held and wanted something different for themselves. The Gen X-ers wanted work-life balance; they longed for it, and it was the first time we started to see this idea of work and life going hand-in-hand.

As members of Generation X became working age, they started to view work as a job, not a lifestyle. A position and title were still desirable and welcome, but they certainly were not worth sweating over. Much like their grandparents (Silent Generation), Gen X-ers would go to work, focus on quality, take initiative when needed but still punch out on time. They wanted to be home with their families. While money is important to the cohort, it is viewed as a means to an end.

Political figures as role models was not something common for most Gen X-ers thanks to Nixon and Clinton. Authority as a whole had a weak presence in the lives of this generation. Parental absenteeism was yet another cause for Gen X-ers to appreciate authority and know it existed, but authority was something of which to be wary. Unlike Baby Boomers who loved sucking up to their bosses, Gen X-ers were often skeptical of their bosses and corporations. To them, work was work.

Are you beginning to see the threads woven throughout history? The Boomers in your corporation are going to work hard, long hours. Quantity of time and dedication to your organization will be there. Quality may or may not. On the other hand, Generation X comes in, and they want to produce good quality work and then leave. To them, work-life balance is critical because they do not want to treat their children the way their parents treated them. That said, if, on occasion, their employer needs them to stick around late or work on a project that takes a bit more time, they will often agree. They want to please their employer. But they do not have to be friends with their employer.

If you employ Gen Xers, they are likely on of your most favorite groups of employees. Yes, they want to maintain a good work-life balance, but they will put in the work they need to do when they need to do it. Typically, they are very loyal. More often than not, they look for a safe and comfortable job.

Gen X-ers are not the ones that are going to pester you for a raise. Most of the time they are very comfortable financially for a number of reasons. The Baby Boomers generated so much financial success and frivolously spent their newly minted cash. As a result, Gen X-ers tasted the luxuries but ultimately longs for quality relationships over materialistic things. Most do not care quite as much — consciously or subconsciously — about earning a high income in their own time, because they know that they will be comfortable throughout their retirement. However, Gen X-ers are also very frugal with their money. They do not need to buy luxury items to prove a point or find their worth.

Gen X-ers were the first generation that saw the shrinking of corporations. General Electric, AT&T, Sears and other big companies — which had become a symbol of job security — were no longer the mammoth corporations that their parents marched off to day in and day out. Of course, these organizations still existed, but they were no longer the picture-perfect example of a secure and stable job.

Traditionally, when someone said they worked for Sears, they were essentially saying they had a safe job and they were going to work there until retirement. With Gen X-ers it started becoming more common to hear people say they were going to work for a medium sized or even small business. Around the same time, there was more of an uptick in entrepreneurialism.

Generation X is responsible for many of the dot-com era successes as well as some of the major technological advances impacting society today.

Cultural Motivators

While the Baby Boomers were seen as dreamers, revolutionaries and world changers, it is often joked that Generation X hated everything. They detested hippies, but also hated corporations. They were not attracted to name brand or conventional fashion, and they are often referred to as the generation without a motto.

In the mid-eighties, this sort of "anti-everything" made way for the grunge scene in both music and fashion. Eighties music amplified this attitude. The band Pearl Jam and lead singer Kurt Cobain of Nirvana were the loudest voices of the grunge movement. The era is marked by thrift-store clothes, big hair and loud accessories.

Truthfully, this generation was wired to challenge authority. For the most part, especially in the workplace, their defiance was silent. Gen X-ers banded together in causes and movements and let their appearance dictate what they stood for.

In 1981, the first case of AIDS was detected in California. In the years afterward, Generation X fought for funding for patient care and AIDS research. During that same time, President Ronald Reagan's administration brought an increasingly conservative political environment. Legalized abortion was under political attack and feminist health clinics became the target of violence. Gen X-ers took to the streets to fight for women's reproductive health, along with LGBT rights. Homosexuality was no longer a topic that was whispered behind closed doors. It took center stage. While the Baby Boomers spurred the Sexual Revolution, Generation X continued it by opening new channels of dialogue that were previously taboo.

In 1991, Clarence Thomas was nominated for a seat on the United States' Supreme Court. That nomination advanced to the Senate Judiciary Committee for the confirmation hearings. Things were going smoothly until law professor, Anita Hill, came forward with accusations that Thomas sexually harassed her when they worked together years prior.

Thomas denied these allegations and was confirmed as an associate justice of the Supreme Court. However, the women of Generation X rallied after the hearing, answering the call of third-wave feminist Rebecca Walker. This was one of the very first times in United States history were women were had a loud voice and the country responded by listening. All of the events that unfolded sparked a surge of women in politics. Many media outlets dubbed the year 1992 as the "Year of the Woman." Many females won elections and took political seats that had historically been held by men.

Innovation

This is the first generation — the first era — that ever had technology that was personal. Technology, as we understand it today, started to have a big influence on this generation. Televisions were no longer one or two per household, some Gen X children had TVs in their rooms. Many families had personal video cameras. It is normal for members of Generation X to have video footage and color photographs of their childhood.

Gen X-ers were the first people that had regular television programming that they could watch, other than news. Not only was there a variety of programming. The programming started to become diverse. For the first time in the 70s and 80s, there were multi-racial television shows. That was a monumental advancement in America's culture.

Baby Boomers were very aware of Martin Luther King, Jr.'s crusade. Many Boomers were just getting their first jobs as the Civil Rights Movement unfolded in the United States. Hollywood saw the trend in the country and began introducing people of different races via TV shows. There were also TV shows that were focused on catering toward different demographic segments. Most Gen X-ers do not remember the days of only all-white sitcoms. Instead, there has always been some level of diversity in media programming for as long as Generation X can remember.

The Baby Boomers saw television and entertainment as an opportunity to revolutionize with civil rights. But it took a whole generation to fully influences the media.

Before 1973, mobile phones were limited to those installed in a vehicle. In the spring of 1973, a Motorola researcher and executive made the first phone call from a handheld mobile phone. These phones offered a thirty-minute talk time and took ten hours to recharge.

In 1984, the Personal Digital Assistant, called a PDA, was born. A newer version, in 1991, had a full keyboard to expand its usability. In general, PDAs stored data, had an appointment calendar, a to-do list function, an address book, a calculator and a memo or note-taking program. The PDA had to be docked to a desktop computer to transfer data.

Mobile phones, personal devices and hand-held technology are just a few of the countless innovations that started to spur technological era today. By the time most members of Generation X purchased their first home, they also had the option for internet. Internet, email and instant messenger programs instantly connected Generation X to the world in a way that had never before been seen.

Many of the older Gen X-ers are responsible for the dot-com boom. Internet startups had soaring prices and tantalizing bullish investors to pour funding into anything with a ".com" or "e-something" in its business plan.

There was so much enthusiasm surrounding the world wide web, but the dot-com boom was followed by the dot-com crash. Investors quickly cut off funding when they saw many startups weren't profitable.

The Recap

This is where you can start to see the cascading effect that really matters — where the events and actions happening in one generation trickle down into the next. Each previous generation's decisions undoubtedly have a direct impact with how the following generation behaves and interacts.

Generation X employees are typically easy to work with and they keep their head down. They do not always trust their managers nor the company for which they work, but all-in-all Gen X-ers make good team members. Being left to fend for themselves and learning how to be resourceful to create school assignments all created a self-starting and responsible generation. Silent Generation members will often view Generation X as disrespectful causing conflict between the two generations in the workplace. Generation X's cynical attitude does not jive with them. Boomers and Gen X-ers generally play nice together in the workplace. Boomers are not intimidated by the average X-er. Boomers are busy trying to further their career and the team member from Generation X just wants a stable job and wants to punch out mostly on time. But, Boomers like Gen X because they are generally dependable and will get the job done right, the first time.

And then you have the Millennials.

Millennials

Born between 1980-2000

Millennials are a different breed.

From the moment they were born, the world was a different place. No, not because of the Millennials, but because of every generation, every historical marker and every innovation that preceded their birth.

Though the culture and climate into which Millennials were born was far different than any previous generation, their attitudes, beliefs and desires are not as far out as you may have once thought. As you read this section of the book, think about what generation Millennials are most similar to — it might actually surprise you.

At the time of this writing, Millennials are generally in their early twenties to late thirties. Many are getting married, potentially buying a home and some are starting families.

From an economic standpoint, Millennials are in their prime spending years. Due to the generation's size and unique way of spending, Millennials are poised to reshape the economy and change the way we buy and sell almost anything. In fact, they already have.

Millennials grew up in a very uncertain time. They grew up much faster than those in previous generations. As we looked at each of the previous generations, most children started grasping adult concepts and perceiving the realities of the world in their late teens to early twenties. Not Millennials. Some psychologists are claiming that Millennials came-of-age as young as eight years-old. Wow! Almost half the age of the previous generation. That is really powerful.

There is one clear reason for this unprecedented exposure to the realities of the world -- technology. For the first time, Millennials had devices they could hold in their hands that tell them what is going on in the world at any given point in time. They visually saw imagery and heard sound bites that no other child in the course of history had before experienced. Millennials had instant connectivity with the rest of the world via instant message, phone call, text, Facebook...you-name-it! It is the profound innovation of this era that allowed Millennials to grow up too fast, yet simultaneously, not fast enough.

Innovation

In a parody video called "The Nature of Millennials", a majority of the myths and rumors swirling around Millennials are brought to light. It jokes that Millennials date only via swiping left or right and that Millennials start their day at noon with avocado toast while simultaneously scrolling through Instagram to see all of the dazzling places their friends are vacationing. Of course, it points out the average three-month job span (not exactly statistically accurate I would like to add). Of course, it all boils down to the fact that this generation is completely shaped by technology.

Technology has arguably advanced more quickly from 1980-2000 than at any other point in all of history. Some argue that the Millennial generation actually stopped in 1996 and a new generation began as technological innovation accelerated even faster at that point.

Where the Baby Boomers would work to amass wealth, Millennials build their entire image using technology. Both generations were focused inwardly on their own self. The Boomers cared about their title and their zip code, whereas the Millennials care about their personal brand, number of followers and average like count.

There are several different kinds of technologies that influenced the speed at which a Millennial learned and soaked up information. For example, this generation is the first generation to have media at their fingertips. Millennials' affinity for technology is also continuing to shape the retail space.

Most in this generation do not know life without a computer or cordless phone. In fact, the second half of the Millennial generation hardly know life without the internet and laptops. But let's get one thing clear. The oldest Millennials are about to turn forty. The cohort is more advanced in age than you might think, so it is important not to get fixated on the young twenty-somethings that are fresh out of college. The label "Millennial" impacts even those that are a bit older.

There are many reasons why the babies of the eighties and nineties are bucketed together. Primarily, it has to do with information accessibility. You see, most houses during these decades had multiple TVs and countless ways to access various channels of coverage in real-time. If you look at Generation X, most of them grew up with one TV per household, sometimes two. By the time the Millennials land on the scene, not only do households average three to four TVs, they simultaneously have about five to seven additional screens in the house.

That means there are almost eight times more screens in the house where an individual could access information— not just the evening news, but programming and information on-demand. Though media devices increased, many in the Millennial generation do not even know what is like to have a corded phone in your room. That rite of passage for so many teenagers (usually Gen-Xers) was replaced with the cordless home telephone. Millennials, unless they went to their grandparents' house, were not used to seeing phones mounted on the wall, where you have to walk around the corner so that your nosy siblings were out of ear shot.

Not only were cordless phones commonplace in homes, Millennials are the first generation that has had access to a phone no matter where they are. No more pay phones. No more phone booths.

It was not until the early 2000s when flip phones and camera phones came into play. Putting a camera on a phone changed the world forever. This innovation unlocked an entirely new cultural phenomenon of capturing events from countless angles and increasing coverage of momentous happenings. Imagine if camera phones had been standard during 9/11. The world would have seen that historical tragedy in a whole new light.

Technology has totally transformed the way in which they've viewed world news and information, which is useful in many ways. But it's also the same way they've been introduced to terror at young ages.

Historical Events

Terror is something that has existed throughout all generations. Typically, it was isolated to wars or conflicts, generally concentrated off-shore. Sadly, Millennials grew up experiencing terror in their own country, possibly their hometowns — they experienced things like the Oklahoma City bombing, which happened in April of 1995.

Anti-government militant Timothy McVeigh parked a truck filled with explosives outside of the Alfred P. Murrah Federal Building in downtown Oklahoma City just before nine in the morning. Because of the explosion, one hundred and sixty-eight people died including nineteen children. It was the worst act of homegrown terrorism in the nation's history.

That is, until the terrorist attacks on September 11, 2001. On that morning, nineteen militants associated with the Islamic extremist group al Qaeda hijacked four airplanes and carried out suicidal attacks targeted toward the Twin Towers of the World Trade Center in New York City, the Pentagon outside of Washington, D.C., and a field in Shanksville, Pennsylvania.

The plane that hit the field was the result of the airplane passengers and flight attendants who fought back against hijackers. Tragically, though no one survived the crash, their bravery likely rerouted the plane, preventing it from attacking one of the suspected targets including the White House, the US Capitol, or the Camp David presidential retreat in Maryland. In total, nearly three thousand people were killed in the attacks.

Not only did the attacks take lives, divide families and cause immense devastation and hurt, the emotional side effects are still healing to this day. After the attacks, anti-Muslim violence in the United States surged. After so many years of racial reconciliation, the Millennials were one of the first generations set-up to get closer to unification. However, racial wounds and tensions were reopened.

Simultaneously, the ripple effects from the September 11 attacks changed Millennials outlook on the world. There was a drastic rise of paranoia and anxiety. People were afraid to leave their homes or go to public places. In fact, several months after the attack, my parents took my brother and I to Walt Disney World in Orlando, Florida. It was a ghost town. We did not have to wait in lines. The park was, at least in Disney terms, empty. People were afraid.

That trip was also the first time I had to go through increased security measures at the airport. No longer were unticketed individuals allowed to meet their loved ones at the gate or watch the planes land from the terminal. The world was changing.

While these incidents were two of many terror-related tragedies Millennials faced in their growing-up year, there were more events that shook their foundation.

Millennials were seeing these things firsthand that had never impacted a generation before. This time, it was happening to families and innocent victims. The news footage following the terrorist attacks was a loop of the towers collapsing, and even people jumping to their deaths as an escape from the burning Towers. No matter where you turned, there was a seemingly uncensored view of what had happened.

For many Millennials, the World Trade Center was more of a patriotic icon that stood for America. Only the very oldest members of the cohort had started their professional jobs, so to many Millennials, the event was slightly distant.

However, one that hit much closer to home was the news footage of another dark day: April 20, 1999. Televisions across the nation aired headlines of the Columbine High School massacre in Columbine, Colorado. Two students entered their high school that morning and brutally killed twelve fellow students and one teacher.

At the time, it was the deadliest school shooting in the nation's history. The twenty-four-hour news cycles perpetuated the fear as they repeated video clips of students running out of their school with their hands clasped behind their heads. Unfortunately, this is an image we have seen many times since then. It is devastating. School violence has become a heartbreaking part of

Millennial culture. Parents feared taking their children to school and the children knew it. Schools implemented active shooter drills.

Growing up, I remember tornado drills and fire drills. They were fun interruptions to class. I longed for these days. Then, one day, I remember "learning" a new drill. The active shooter drill or the shelter in place drill as it is now more commonly referred to. This drill was not as entertaining. It became more serious. My mind was filled with what ifs… it certainly did not help that during my senior year of high school, a student actually brought a handgun to campus. Thankfully he was caught and as the story goes, there was no malintent, he just wanted to show it off to his friends.

Bomb threats also became a real thing. Multiple times throughout middle school and high school, our school was evacuated or on lockdown. Localized and isolated terror incidents on US soil, whether senseless teenage violence or horrific convoluted crusades, became normal—well as normal as horrific events like this could be.

After the shooting at Columbine, there was a shift in the way people talked about bullying and school violence. Today, the two are seen as linked. Much of society blamed exclusive social cliques, alternative music, action movies and video games for teen violence. While varying arguments can be made for what causes these tragic outbursts, one truth remains: witnessing senseless violence has almost become normal for Millennials.

Many schools have implemented heavy security measures to prevent future incidents. Some methods include hiring security guards surrounding school buildings, students being required to wear uniforms, implementation of clear backpacks, and metal detectors acting as the gateway between the outside world and the school. Police officers have also assessed their tactics for handling school shootings, and the conversation surrounding gun control legislation comes up after any similar form of on-campus violence.

For many previous generations, tragedy had been relatively isolated. Of course, news broadcasts included major incidents, but maybe just for a news cycle or two. Further, with every generation prior to Millennials there was limited way to interact with a news story. If you wanted to talk to your friends about what you had just seen or heard, you would do so in person the next day at school or you would have to call them on them phone—that is if your sister was not on a three-way call with her best friends gossiping and jamming up the phone line.

Millennials not only saw these events unfold, they are the first generation that could instantly communicate, voice their opinion and share the stories with friends as the new unfolded. Social media exacerbated the impact of tragedy. Instead of being able to talk about news stories with parents, who inevitably had the emotional maturity to walk their children through trials, the Millennials turned to their adolescent, hormonally charged peers. This caused raw emotion to be unfiltered and posted for the world to see every time tragedy struck.

Social Media

As the Gen Z Millennials (those born in the 1990s) hit their already confusing tween years, social media started dominating the social landscape. The earlier born Millennials were in college at the time of the social media boom. Starting in 2002, the internet was the launchpad of several social media platforms, each having an individual impact on their audiences.

March 2002: Friendster is launched. Friendster has since been sold and is now a gaming website, but it made its debut as a social networking site that allowed users to contact other users and share online content with them.

December 2002: LinkedIn is launched. LinkedIn is a professional networking platform for businesses and employment-oriented services.

August 2003: MySpace is founded. MySpace was the largest social networking site in the world from 2005-2008. It allowed users to create personal profiles and share blogs, photos, music and videos. Anyone could become an artist and gain followers. With the subsequent launch of YouTube, many would teach themselves guitar or piano to become their own rockstar.

February 2004: Facebook goes live. Facebook is a popular social networking site that allows users to create profiles, upload photos and videos, and send messages. Mark Zuckerberg's story of an overnight billionaire resonated with so many millions and movies like *The Social Network* romanticized the Silicon Valley start-up life. Rock stars were now not the only type of celebrity worth aspiring to be like.

February 2005: YouTube is born. YouTube is a video sharing site, which was purchased by Google in 2006 for $1.65 billion. It rivals its parent company's chief product, Google, as one of the largest search engine platforms. This unlocked a new way to learn how to fix things around the house, teach yourself new skills and access quick entertainment in ninety seconds.

June 2005: Reddit is launched. Reddit is a social news aggregation and discussion website where registered users can submit content. This further promoted the idea that stories could be discussed online with complete strangers.

March 2006: Twitter goes live. Twitter is a microblogging and social networking service where users post and interact with each other using messages called "Tweets." Twitter has had a checkered past. In its early years it was the standard for building a personal brand. Only the most elite could have the blue verified badge. Now, Twitter has converted more into a breaking news site. Celebrities are less present than they used to be and now the blue tick is reserved for news personalities and journalists to help eliminate "fake news."

October 2008: Spotify goes live. Spotify is an audio-streaming platform where users can create and share playlists. A year before its release, Apple released the iPhone. Though MP3 players had existed, the notion of buying a song instead of an album did not really take off until the iPhone. Simultaneously, streaming services, like Spotify, made music social. You could instantly get access to new songs and albums for a low monthly cost and you could share playlists with friends making music social again.

March 2010: Pinterest is launched. Pinterest is a software designed to enable discovering and saving online information in a visual way. YouTube helped catalyze the do-it-yourself (DIY) movement but Pinterest solidified it. Millennials are extremely crafty as a whole. They want picture-perfect decorations, crafts, costumes, outfits, etc. Pinterest spurred on the inner artist in many Millennials.

October 2010: Instagram is launched. Instagram is a photo-sharing app and a social network platform that allows users to upload and edit photos and short videos. Originally only available on iPhone, Instagram, out of the gate, created an elitist mentality. The idea of influencers was truly born out of Instagram. A photo speaks a thousand words and that was the goal with this platform. Millennials started posting only the best of the best of their lives—vacations, cars, houses, fine dining, beverages, private jets. The platform evoked a world of luxury. Consequently, I am honored to have one of those blue verified check marks next to my name on Instagram.

July 2011: SnapChat is born. SnapChat is a mobile messaging app used to share photos, videos, text and drawings that disappear within a set time frame after opening. In the hands of adolescents whose brains are clearly not fully firing on all cylinders (my professional opinion), having disappearing images caused major chaos. A rise in sexually explicit imagery caused new waves of bullying. Minors were photographing themselves inappropriately. And yes, while the image disappears, in seconds, it only takes seconds to screenshot the image and wreak havoc.

The data in 2019 shows that social media platforms have a little more than three billion daily active users, which is about forty-two percent of the population. Millennials make up the majority of those users — ninety percent of the Millennials surveyed were daily users. Seventy-eight percent were Gen X-ers and forty-eight percent were Baby Boomers.

In 2018, it was reported that Facebook and YouTube were the most popular social media channels among Millennials and an average of two hours a day were spent on social media. If you look at the latter half of Millennials, those primarily born in the nineties, you see Instagram and YouTube being the more predominant channel.

By using various forms of social media, Millennials have always been able to easily see what their friends are doing. They are very aware of what their friends are posting online. Unfortunately, many get this fake view of what the world should be. In turn, many Millennials take their peers social media presence as litmus test for what their life should be like.

More than ever, there is an increasing gap of reality versus what could be. This is because their friends — and millions of people they don't know —

have posted their lives online. Social media allows anyone to create their own brand and be whomever they want to be.

Instead of being inundated by horrifying images, social media has helped Millennials quickly learn the art of putting their best foot forward. Online, there are no bad days. Instead, life is simply beautiful. Social media is a ploy for Millennials to get instant gratification and affirmation by acquiring the most "likes" on their photos.

Social media caused a dramatic shift. All of the sudden, Millennials are no longer thinking of friends as the group at the lunch table. Say goodbye to jock, goth, burnouts and the preps. Enter foodies, travelers, explorers, fashionistas, bloggers and influencers. Now, friends are the ones that interact with them online.

For the first time, because of technology, cross-country moves no longer separated friends from each other. Distance became relative. Cell phones, texting, mobile internet, and social media has shrunk the world unlike ever before.

While these major technological advances helped the world become more unified, expanded diversity and inclusion as well as created community, it came with loads of baggage. Millennials were getting bullied. It was not by the big kid pushing them around and stuffing them in a locker. Instead, they were getting abused with words via social media.

People, and when I say that I mean Millennials, could hide behind the disguise of an online profile — real or not. Then they started to abuse media. With free, easy apps and platforms, anyone could create an entire life online that may or may not exist anywhere else. This has shaped the way this generation perceives everything. Truths became relative.

The online, social media culture has created a highly competitive market for Millennials. Millennials wanted to antagonize their virtual friend following by going to fun, exotic destinations and having epic vacations — mostly to get the pictures. Millennials are avid consumers lavishly spending money on anything that is picture worthy. Marketers, take note.

As a whole, the generation's desires to cast an image of themselves that portrays them as popular and famous and fun. In creating a bulletproof digital persona, Millennials feel as if they are shielding the world from the ability so that no one can criticize their lifestyle choices. That is why FyreFestival worked. Social media has lured Millennials and even their families on vacations and excursions around the globe. No adventure is too outlandish if it means getting the opportunity to take great pictures to share online.

Millennials are not lured by the idea of accumulating stuff. The Baby Boomers were. This is an interesting distinction between otherwise similarly self-focused generations. Instead, they want to have experiences and seek adventures that allow them to seize the moment. They crave access more than ownership, which seeps into other areas of like, such as why they rent apartments in cities instead of buying a home in the suburbs.

For this generation, it is all about having a unique experience and being able to share it with others. Currently, sixty-five percent of Millennials are saving their money to travel, and seventy-two percent of this group says they would rather spend their money on experiences over material items. Again, this is an anecdote all managers and marketers should note. An experience is far more important to Millennials than even money.

It was not that long ago — about ten years or so — when we all had to to take our disposable cameras or rolls of film to the drugstore and get them developed. These envelopes of photos likely would not see the light of day unless someone came over and we showed them the scrapbook from that annual Florida vacation with the entire family.

It is not just about vacations, it is also about extravagant marriage proposals, bridal showers, baby announcements, gender reveals, and even "Prom-posals" — high schoolers asking each other to prom in ways that rival wedding proposals on "The Bachelor." Millennials consume others' experiences and feel forced to constantly keep up and compare. Keeping up with the Jones' has a whole new meaning.

Millennials are equally self-confident and utterly insecure. They assign their worth to a number of followers, fans and likes. They are social. Generally speaking, Millennials are obsessed with what others think of them. That is why not receiving a trophy is devastating for a Millennial, they feel as if they have failed. While they confidently post pictures of their personal lives, food, clothes, bodies, vacations, cars and homes, they are insecure beyond measure. This confidence and timidness is held in an odd tension.

Interestingly enough, this desire to be loved drives a high level of morals. Millennials are exceedingly aware that their dirt can quickly be aired to the world. As a result, Millennials are often more careful to adhere towards societal morals. Now, these are not necessarily their grandparents' morals. More typically they try to conform to the standards of their peers.

Education

Schools, which were a place of learning and a mandate from the Gen X parents, became a place to be afraid after Columbine. Cities and American icons like the Twin Towers were attacked making travel and busy places scary. This created an "every person for themselves" mentality. Anxiety skyrocketed. In fact, some refer to Millennials as the Therapy Generation. Social media had a large role to play as well.

This is a generation that is afraid of going to school because of what their friends might think of them after they posted a picture last night of their gourmet dinner and received a disapproving comment from one of their digital friends. Add in the presence of terror along with the instant, constantly breaking, real-time feel of news and social media, and there's pressure from all angles.

Over the past several years, as Millennials enter adulthood, research has found a forty-seven percent increase in mental health diagnosis within the cohort compared to previous cohorts. On one hand, this is excellent. Awareness of mental health challenges have been brought into the spotlight. Instead of being ashamed of some very real and serious issues, Millennials are more confident and equipped to seek help. That said, the increase is not solely due to more awareness and acceptance of seeking out a mental health professional. A large part of the increase is undoubtedly connected to online bullying, social media influences and the constant exposure to frightening circumstances.

Tragically, the suicide rate in the United States is on a steady incline of about two percent a year. While mental health has become a focal point for Millennials, there is still a tremendous amount of work that must be done. A recent study conducted by the Wall Street Journal cites that the average Millennial spends about $3,600 each year on self-help resources, professional counseling and personal growth initiatives. This figure includes activities like yoga and meditation classes.

As if the Millennials did not have enough social and political pressures in their formative years, they were also ridiculously busy. Many Millennials are used to a full schedule that includes much more than just going to school. As the school bell rings at three o'clock, the typical Millennial is just starting their day — they have soccer practice, rehearsal for drama, jump rope practice, chess lessons or another parent-induced activity.

This is probably the most well-rounded generation in all of history. The seemingly endless opportunities for extracurriculars as well as a much more refined education system position Millennials for optimal experiences and success. From a historical perspective, this is the first generation to forget that education is a gift. With acts such as No Child Left Behind in 2001 and more robust curriculum, nearly even child in America was being educated. Education by the Millennial generation is often taken for granted.

College, for most, is now just a part of the educational experience, it is an entitlement. College is also a bragging right. Undergraduate degrees are expected. For many Millennials, graduate degrees were no longer seen as "extra" — for many career paths, secondary degrees were necessary.

This exceedingly high level of education did not just blossom from nowhere. It was cultivated as young as grade school for many in the generation. For the first time, Millennials had their own schedules. Parents wanted to be over involved in the lives of their children.

Welcome to the era of Helicopter Parents.

Home Life

Baby Boomers with Millennial children often wanted their children to be the best that they could be. Children to Boomers were a trophy. Comparing their child's grades and performance in various activities was a badge of honor. This caused this group of parents to put immense pressure on their children. Undoubtedly, this incredible weight placed on performance and appearances was difficult for Millennials to understand as children. They would strive to make their parents proud and in turn, often developed an unhealthy people-pleasing mentality.

The Boomers typically had children a bit later as they were so focused on their careers. That said, it was not uncommon for Boomers and Gen X-ers to have children around the same time. Often a Boomer's youngest child would be the same age as a Gen X-ers oldest child. This caused a unique blend of generational influences on the Millennials.

Generation X also had their own version of Helicopter Parenting. Since Gen X-ers grew up coming home from school with no one home, they wanted something different for their children. They wanted to break the cycle of Latch Key kids. So, they overprogrammed their Millennial children. Boomers were more likely to have their kids in programs where they could excel and thrive and be bragging right at a cocktail party. Gen X parents of Millennial children often bragged on the business of their kids. Simultaneously, Gen X parents were often far more involved in their children's lives and schools. They were lunch moms and baseball coaches. Since careers were not quite as important to Gen X-ers as they were to Boomers, you see a high level of Gen X parent involvement.

If you think about it, Millennials were the first generation where they had their own schedules. Parents work schedules became eclipsed by soccer, dance, football, band and theater.

Scheduling was not the only profound impact that parents of Millennials had on their children. Parents were more concerned about being friends than parents. The authoritarian version of parenting that had existed started to fade away. Particularly Gen X parents of Millennials desired this close and intimate friendship with their children. They wanted to make up for the absenteeism of their parents. So, they overcorrected. In fact, it is very hard to find Gen X parents that disciplined their children. Why? Because they wanted to show love to their precious little snowflakes. Most parents of Millennials cannot stand to have disapproval from their children. Boomers hate it because Boomers long for approval. Gen X-ers hate the disapproval because they want to provide a better life for their children than they felt they had received while growing up.

This is where it gets interesting. Most Millennials have lost all sense of authority because now Millennials are thinking, "My parents were my friends and they are the oldest people that I know intimately. So, if the only authority-ish figure that I have is my friend, then all authority figures should talk to me, treat me and love me like a friend."

But then there were coaches. Coaches, directors, mentors, yogis, whatever it might be were also authority figures for Millennials. However, coaching shifted dramatically during the Millennials' upbringing. Parents would lose it if their child was mistreated. Again, this goes to a lack of discipline and a more friendly approach to child rearing. When coaches yelled at the child, momma bear would yell louder at the coach. Yet another example of Helicopter Parenting.

So, the parents forced coaches to morph from the tough love, run until you puke, drill sergeants to mentors and encouragers and motivators.

A shift happened. Coaches, instead of kicking the football players' cans when things were not going right, became more friendly and more loving and more supporting. Now, coaches started to also become more like friends. As you can see that across the board, Millennials have new view on relationships.

Attitudes Towards Work and Finances

From Helicopter Parents to the prying eyes of their social friends, Millennials are so used to their lives being examined under a microscope. As a result, the generation typically has a higher moral code. More often than not, they are fearful of doing bad things. They desire the affirmation and affection and approval of authority figures. They always kept busy as children with coaches and teachers and if they failed to get a trophy, they felt like personal failures.

When it comes to work, Millennials are unique. They saw YouTube star Susan Boyle win Britain's Got Talent and Justin Bieber become an overnight popstar. Millennials saw Mark Zuckerberg launch a social network that redefined the world all while amass billions of dollars and fans.

Millennials, having always received trophies (or something equivalent), possess an odd balance of optimism and realism. Of course, Millennials desire stardom and endless wealth. It is not secret they want approval. But contrary to what most believe about the generation, they are relatively realistic. While they optimistically desire to do these things, the are also very self-aware and realize that they may get their break but should enjoy life right now.

The "right now" factor comes as a result of instant gratification. Instant gratification comes as a result of technology. This outlook on life has changed the way in which the generation views work and money. Millennials typically work to spend. A job is simply a means to an end. They earn so they can go on a lavish vacation and post it on social media.

Interestingly enough, Millennials are less likely to buy houses and expensive cars and instead are more likely to invest in a metal credit card and a ride on a private jet or a yacht…at least for the photo op. Hundreds of thousands of dollars spent on life's luxuries over thirty years is far more important to most Millennials than a house worth the same amount. Especially if their self-indulgence makes for a great photo shoot for Instagram.

Millennials have been putting off life milestones, such as marriage or buying a house. Shocker, I know. A growing number of Millennials are choosing to live with their parents instead. Since they saw the world and its true colors from an unfortunately young age, Millennials have grown comfortable cozying up in their parents' basements.

To prove this fact, though I doubt you needed proof, in 2010, thirty percent of eighteen to thirty-four years old were living with their parents. Their parents were already married by that point, had a house and were planning for children. The average Millennial is now waiting to get married until about the age of thirty. That is more than half a decade later than their parents.

The experiential lifestyle and the comforts of home not only has skewed the view of finances and family but has had a profound impact on a Millennial's outlook on work.

To Millennials, work is a gig. It occupies time between Monday and

Friday. Millennials are also used to the "gig economy." The gig economy is made up of companies such as Uber, Lyft, Upwork, Fiverr...the list goes on. These gigs are basically any job that gives you the freedom and flexibility to work when, where and how you want. Millennial's chaotic upbringing and constant go-go-go has amplified their desire for flexibility. But contrary, being sheltered from bills, housing and other adulting-type tasks, has caused them to need structure. While they desire freedom, they cannot function without structure.

Cultural Motivators

Millennials are cause driven. They have strayed away from the ideas of large non-profit organizations and instead have focused on the idea of a cause. A cause can be followed. A cause has a personality and a mission and an identity.

As a result of being able to see the world with all of its warts and scars, Millennials want to initiate change. Though Millennials are often touted as self-centered, they do have a large desire to be philanthropic. Arguably, it may be because it is trendy to care and caring makes them look good, but nevertheless, they do care.

According to the 2017 Millennial Impact Report, some of the top causes Millennials are passionate about include the environment, college and post-secondary education, poverty and homelessness, mental health and social services, criminal justice reform, women's rights, healthcare and reproductive care, early education, and sexual-orientation-based rights. Millennials care.

This generation is passionate about issues, not institutions. More than ninety percent of Millennials say they would stop giving to an organization if they began distrusting it.

In fact, seventy-three percent of Millennials volunteer regularly for a non-profit. What is even more fascinating is that nearly four out of every five Millennials prefer giving of their time and money to a cause, not a non-profit. This generation clearly distinguishes between the two, though in reality they are mostly the same.

Millennials are more likely than members of previous generations to make point-of-sale donations, gather their friends to attend charity events and purchase products or services from companies that lend their profits to a worthy cause. Nearly fifty percent currently give monthly online to a cause that they support.

Generations Y, Z... and iGen

Most experts divide the Millennial generation up into two groups: Generation Y, which is the first decade of the Millennial generation born between 1981-1990. The second wave of Millennials, Generation Z is from 1990-2000, and each group has their own set of unique characteristics. It would be easy to fill the remaining pages with the differences amongst Millennials. However, for simplicity sake, we will explore the two distinct cohorts together. There are enough similarities between the parents and children of this era to lump them altogether as Millennials.

Remember, there is a generational blur as well. While historians make clean cuts between generations on January first of a given year, the reality is generational lines are bit fuzzy based on countless external factors. That said, nearly everyone agrees that the Millennial cohort ends right around the year 2000.

The new millennia brought about a new generation.

iGeneration is the generation born in 2000 and after. iGen is a smaller generational cohort than the Millennials, and although we are still learning about them, they will likely have similarities with the Silent generation, or the Traditionalists.

Generation Y

Individuals in Generation Y and Z are similar, but there are a few things that set them apart from each other. Gen Y were in grade school when the

Columbine tragedy happened in 1999. Because of that, they saw the change in school, going from an innocent time to later practicing "school shooter" drills.

This generation did have their own phones, but they were Nokia or Motorola flip phones — not smartphones — and they didn't get them until the end of high school or even college. At that time, phone plans didn't include text messaging, and any type of texting was done through a numerical keypad.

They also remember VCR — how life was before DVR and TV streaming services — record stores, the Walkman, CD players, and boomboxes, but they didn't grow up with ready access to computers.

Because of that, members of Gen Y are often better at spelling and grammar since they didn't have word processing programs to rely on. They are said to collaborative and creative in the workplace. This group also likely got financial help from their parents when they went to college, which is foreign to Gen Z.

As far as pop culture goes, Gen Y saw 80's movies and have cult favorites from the 90's. By the time Disney was remaking all of their classic films, Gen Y was too old to see them.

Generation Z

Members of Generation Z were in grade school when the terror attacks happened on September 11, 2001. They have always traveled under the strict regulations brought forth post-September 11.

By the time Gen Z got their drivers' licenses, they already had iPhones and were regularly texting — which was now built-in to phone plans — and they have never experienced having a mobile phone without being able to text.

Gen Z also uses their phones for GPS. In fact, this group has likely never seen traditional GPS that was a device all on its own, because they've always had it available through a phone app.

This generation grew up with regular access to computers, and they are often prolific writers because they have already had so much communication via texting and typing. However, Gen Z is not considered to be as eloquent orally as someone from Gen Y.

By the time Gen Z was preparing for college, their parents had many more expenses — from the latest technology to extravagant vacations — and for most Gen Z-ers, there was no college fund. Gen Z Millennials often struggle with student debt from college-related expenses for many years after earning a degree.

In general, this group is seen as realistic, financially savvy and ultra-connected. Gen Z Millennials are the ones attending all of the Disney movie reboots, because the originals were such a staple for them, and they are slowly starting to have children.

As you can see, there are some differences between these groups, but they are still Millennials and it's safe to say they would benefit from the managing and motivating tactics offered in the next section of the book. These differences, although subtle, may simply offer additional insight into the Millennials in your world.

For example, a Gen Z Millennial will not get any of your movie references from the 80's, and Gen Y employees won't really relate to *Pocahontas* or *The Lion King* movie lines. They are all products of Generation X and they all have been incredibly programmed by their Helicopter Parents.

iGen

The Millennials have similarities with Gen X-ers, and it's expected that iGen will be more materialistic. They don't know life before a flat screen TV, they don't know life without internet in their hand — we're not even talking about wireless internet, we are talking about internet in the palm of their hand in a phone.

They do not know life without being about to call anywhere in the world for just about free, they do not know about calling cards that you used to buy at Target and things like that. They have totally changed everything.

iGen has just seen things in a totally different way. They do not even know that Blockbuster ever existed or that you could go get a movie anywhere, but hitting stream, I want it now.

The interesting thing is, college is becoming increasingly less important. Think about it, their parents — the Millennials — were so burdened with student debt and may not have gotten a job that fully utilized their degree. There is a higher need for trade skills, combined with the increase in technology and automation, we may see iGen jump on that shift.

So, if you think the Millennials want it now, just wait until the iGen gets to the workforce.

PART TWO:

Managing and Motivating Millennials

Millennial Myths

By 2025, it is predicted that Millennials will make up as much as seventy-five percent of the world's working population. This is why it is becoming vital for business leaders and managers to better understand how to manage this large —and sometimes confusing — generation.

Since Millennials hit the scene, there have been so many rumors and myths swirling around them — that they want constant praise, they feel entitled, they are lazy, they have an obsession with technology, they lack social etiquette — the list goes on and on.

As with any myth or stereotype, there usually is an element of truth to it. However, the label is often formed because of our own experiences. Our interaction then influences the subconscious lens we are using to analyze someone.

You may have picked up this book just for this section--that is totally fine. I trust there are nuggets you can glean from reading through some of the common Millennial myths. With that said, if you did skip over Part I of this book, "The Generations," you will be unable to fully grasp the leadership lessons in the pages ahead. Though there is a great deal of history in the first half of this text, it truly is the foundation by which you will be able to build your management strategies for dealing with Millennials. In fact, I would argue that if you just read the first section of this book, you are equipped well enough that you could stop reading here, though I hope that you do continue.

Let's explore some of these common Millennial myths and get to the truth behind them.

MYTH 1: Millennials Are Entitled

Over my career, I have managed many, many different Millennials. Oh wait, I am a Millennial myself. Though my birth year locks me into this generation, I would argue, as would many that know me, that I am a generational mutt. My circumstances growing up and those who influenced and mentored me throughout my life. So sadly, I would say that my own generation does sometimes make me hang my head in shame. On the other hand, many times, I understand the why behind most of a Millennial's actions and attitudes.

One of the most consistent questions (well they are really complaints) that I receive is about Millennials being entitled. Managers cry out, "They need constant praise...they always ask for raises...they need affirmation."

My answer, "Yes." Millennials are seemingly a bit more sensitive, needy and entitled. But many of those labels are just the tip of the iceberg—in reality there is an underlying problem as we will explore.

I have lost count of the number of Millennials I have interviewed for jobs opportunities over the years—probably hundreds. On more than one occasion, a Millennial would walk into their interview and say, "Hey, when am I going to get my first raise?"

Every time, I have to pick my jaw up off the floor. In my mind I am thinking, "You haven't even started yet. Why do you need a raise?"

How entitled is someone that walks into a situation where they are vying for a job and the first thing they care about is how much they get paid and when they will get paid more? It is absurd. The Silent Generation just wanted a job and stability. Baby Boomers wanted raises but would work hard to earn one. Generation X wanted to just get through the work week, be comfortable but have a sense of work life balance. The past generations wanted stability, hard work and comfort, respectively. And then you have the Millennial, "Gimme, gimme, gimme" before they even have an offer letter. What gives?

You have to wonder why a Millennial would ask for a raise prior to starting a job. Why would anyone do that?

Let's break this down. What is a *raise* to a Millennial?

Jokes aside, to a Millennial, a raise is a trophy. Of course, it is a bit stereotypical to say that every Millennial wants a trophy, but the reality is there is some truth behind it. No, they do not need a cheap gold-coated figurine on a faux-marble pedestal with their name engraved on it. Instead, they are wanting a milestone. Yes, a trophy represents affirmation, and we will cover that momentarily. However, more than a feel-good moment, a trophy embodies everything a Millennial has worked for up to a certain point.

Think about it, for their entire lives, the Millennials have always worked towards the next milestone. Whether a grade, a concert, a play, a game, a degree, another degree, this generation has always worked towards a goal and received affirmation upon completion. A grade appears on a report card, a concert and play end in applause, a game ends in a victory and a degree ends in a diploma.

Millennials, when it comes to project management, tasks and even the flow of life, are very driven by concrete examples and clear goals. With a clear goal must come a defined outcome. That outcome must be measurable.

So in a job interview, when a Millennial is asking about raises or a career path or what their next promotion is, they are simply asking what they must do to be successful.

Too often, managers take this request early on in a job interview process as entitlement. Consequently, leaders are often turned off by a Millennial's boldness in asking such a question that they pass over a perfectly qualified candidate.

Most of the time, when a Millennials asks one of these promotion or raise type questions, they are not entirely concerned with time. While time is a factor, what is more important to a Millennial is a clear path with goals and objectives to a given promotion, raise or move up in their career.

Believe it or not, if well thought out, many Millennials are okay with waiting for a raise if they know what milestones they must hit to deserve the honor of a new position. Beware, Millennials are exceedingly motivated though, so they may reach your goals more quickly than you had anticipated. You better believe, the moment that they check all of your boxes, they will come knocking at your door with their hand out expecting their reward.

The entitlement label thrust upon Millennials is not isolated to merely promotions and pay raises. Their desire for attention, status and constant approval often contributes to them earning the tag as an utterly entitled youngin'.

The reality is, Millennials seek affirmation more than any generation that has come before them. So rest assured, you are not going crazy when thinking Millennials are a bit more needy than their predecessors.

That said, if you look at the Baby Boomers, they were pretty needy too. That more mature generation is characterized by being very materialistic. The Boomers often looked for affirmation by purchasing things, having a large house, a fancy car, the best clothes, and name-brand items. The big difference, a Boomer had a different work ethic and would work long hours to earn their so-called trophies. Arguably, quantity of time was prioritized by Boomers more than quality of work for most Boomers.

Generational Perceptions

This is a huge rub in the workplace today. Millennials can work faster than their predecessors. Technology comes naturally and even the ability to self-teach and learn new tasks comes more quickly to this young generation. Often, Millennials can complete a job at a higher level of quality in a significantly shorter amount of time than a Boomer. Secretly, that drivers many Boomers batty. More on this to come in a later chapter.

We see that same approval-seeking with the Millennial generation; however we see it take a new form. It is true, Millennials need approval from others, which is part of the reason they are so addicted to social media. But they also want to be recognized by their office superiors and their peer coworkers.

Millennials are not as entitled as many believe. They will work for the carrot dangled in front of them. It is often not about money. By the number of times they ask for raises, it is easy to assume they are obsessive about their paycheck. Instead of rolling your eyes at another request, view this as a cry for affection.

The truth is, Millennials are more interested in authentic value brought on by the work itself, learning new things and meeting interesting people. Millennials want to feel and know they are valued, too. Affirmation is important.

When a Millennial asks for a raise, a red flag should go up in the minds of all managers. The individual could be discontent with their work environment or under appreciated. Maybe the Millennial checked all the boxes for a raise you promised them at an earlier point. They will be waiting at your door to collect their upgrade.

Millennials had constant feedback with their parents, coaches, teachers and authority figures their entire life. When this, sometimes weekly, feedback all of a sudden moves to once a year during an annual review, Millennials get fearful. As people pleasers, they are concerned they are not living up to their boss's expectations. Instead of walking in their manager's office, closing the door and asking how they are performing, they walk in and ask for a raise. A raise is the carrot that has been dangled in front of a Millennial as a badge of achievement.

You can curb the constant financial merit requests by simply infusing positive feedback into your workplace. Over time, Millennials will mature and likely will need less constant affirmation. However, in the interim, you may have to meet them halfway.

Even when you ask a Millennial to do a regular part of their job — whether that be taking out the trash or pulling weekly reports — and you should thank them for it.

I know, I know, that is part of their job. I agree that as a manager you should not have to go out of your way to thank them for doing the bare minimum of what they are paid to do. But make it a priority at least once a week to say something encouraging to your younger team members.

If only it were that easy. Millennials are sensitive and are used to generic praise. On social media, they get blown up with generic comments about how yummy their food looks. Quantity at that point counts. When it comes to a leader or authority figure in the workplace it is a quality comment that is more significant.

"Good job" and "great work" help encourage a Millennial, but those remarks can often be too generic. Instead, if you say, "Hey, thanks for taking out the trash..." — and then, if you are feeling so compelled, tell a story about how their action helped to make a difference. Connecting a Millennial's action to the greater good will help encourage them and make them feel truly appreciated in your work environment.

It is important to know, Millennials are young too. And they are more emotionally immature than previous generations. Some of these ideas are simply best practices for young team members. Yes it may seem absurd that you need to seemingly treat Millennials with kid-gloves, but if it saves you having to keep increasing salaries to keep around the majority of your workforce, it may just be worth considering.

While a request for a raise could be a red flag of job dissatisfaction, there is another, external force, pressuring Millennials into begging for a pay bump. Of course, we all need a salary to pay our bills. Millennials are not immune to that. They cannot all go mine bitcoin on demand.

Millennials are Strapped Financially

That said, a request for a raise may stem from a point of financial desperation. Millennials have an interesting relationship with money. It is very possible likely that these Millennial employees literally cannot afford their basic necessities: internet, streaming services, cell phone service. Oh, then there is food clothing and shelter too. Let's not forget school loans.

Millennials are the first generation to have added "utilities" to their life.

Most have a laptop, a TV, a tablet, a cell phone, internet service and cell phone subscriptions as a normal part of living expenses. Taking the hardware out (the laptop, TV, tablet and cell phone), most Americans are paying about $140.00 each and every month for just internet and cell phone connectivity. Add in video streaming services, cell phone payment plans, rent, utilities, transportation and food, you are talking about a steep increase in cost of living compared to previous generations.

That does not even include frivolous monthly subscription expenses for things like organic food and wine delivery, music streaming, clothing and jewelry shipments, subscription dog food and toys, Amazon Prime Membership and so many more. As many as seventy percent of Millennials have at least one recurring delivery.

Millennials are attracted to subscriptions and other small bits of luxury they cannot afford, partly because these delivery services are convenient. Millennials are busy with their social lives and food delivery saves time. Budgeting is something many Millennials did not see clearly outlined for them. So, when a Millennial can have a fixed cost such as a delivery service, they can roll into their list of expenses. Subscription services have also made it possible for Millennials to avoid commitment — more on this later — because they can skip weeks or months without penalty.

Aside from subscription services and luxury items, there is also a very real issue of student debt. Millennials are the first generation ever to experience student debt on such an individual level.

There are a few reasons for this. Parents of Millennial children often wanted to help their kids with tuition fees, but higher education is much more expensive today than it was decades ago. On average, tuition costs are more than four times what Generation X had to pay to attend college.

The cost of tuition, and room and board at four-year colleges has increased by sixty-eight percent since the 1999-2000 academic year. The amount of money borrowed annually has doubled since then. According to the numbers from the second quarter of the 2019 fiscal year, there were approximately $498 billion in outstanding student loan debt for 15 million borrowers. That averages $33,000 for each borrower.

The majority of parents were not prepared to save enough money monthly to amass a nest egg that could cover the sharp increases in tuition. As a result, many Millennials paid for part or all of their higher education out of pocket or rather with the help of Uncle Sam and the banks. The consequence of accumulating six figures in debt before being legal drinking age have left the average Millennial owing anywhere between $400-$1,500 owed per month in school-related debt.

In order to afford just schooling, an employee would have to be making a post-tax annual salary of $18,000. Of course, there is also rent. The average rent in the United States for a two-bedroom apartment clocks in at $1,082 per month (if you are lucky). If you get a job in a city, which is the case for many Millennials, you are paying even more. The average one-bedroom in New York City as of the April 2019, will run an average of $2,945 per month.

New York City aside, adding the average school loan payment to the average rent payment across the United States, a Millennial would need a minimum post-tax annual salary of $30,000 to have shelter. Pre-taxes, that is around a $40,000 starting salary. Now that does not seem too unreasonable. Think again. That does not include food, transportation, clothing, entertainment, healthcare, additional debt, cell phone, internet, savings, etc. Millennials have high expenses. In order to have even a taste of the lifestyle they grew up with, Millennials require higher starting salaries than previous generations because there are just more expenses to be covered.

If a Millennial is not being compensated fairly in their eyes, they are going to let their employer know. Sometimes it has to do with job dissatisfaction. At other times, Millennials, on their own for the first time, are desperately trying to make ends meet. Those numbers and statistics are just for Millennials that received an undergraduate degree. Millennials who earned a postgraduate degree often have even higher expense.

What does all of this mean for managers? With more than seventy-five percent of Gen Z Millennials believing they should be promoted in their first year on the job, you are bound to have one in your office asking for some sort of upgrade.

While their impatience can be frustrating, it is important to remember that this generation was given permission to go for it from every adult in their life. They were told to ask for what they wanted -- to take risks. That is actually quite an admirable quality most Millennials possess. That said, it must be channeled properly and used to an organization's advantage.

Alternatives to Monetary Raises

If a monetary raise is out of the question, whether because the employee does not deserve increased compensation or because of company finances, there is still an opportunity. Remember, Millennials want recognition and affirmation, but more than that, they desire structure. They want clear goals and milestones that they can work towards to get the trophy. Between the carrot and the stick, Millennials will almost always run for the carrot and almost always shut down with the stick.

One practical way to try to deal with the seemingly entitled Millennial that wants a promotion or a raise is to take an introspective look into your organization. Is there a way you can better recognize employees when they reach certain milestones?

You may also consider offering more frequent feedback to your Millennial employees, such as quarterly instead of annually. Talk with them about planning a realistic career path and show them how this job will help them get there. Provide opportunities for them to learn new skills that could lead them to a promotion. If their job role has shifted during their time at the office, maybe a new job title is in order.

Many businesses have started rewarding employees on their work anniversaries with small tokens of appreciation such as a company lunch, a gift card, or even their picture on the company's social media page. Perhaps a work anniversary brings a few extra PTO days or the opportunity for flex work time. These are all trophies a Millennial would be proud to receive. The more specific and personalized, the better. If you can specifically and publicly praise a Millennial for value that they have added to your organization as a whole, you will have them eating out of the palm of your hand.

TRUTH: Millennials seek recognition from their superiors and coworkers. They want to be recognized for their hard work, including tasks that are expected of them on the job. Millennials also carry the burden of student debt, and often need a higher base salary to cover basic expenses.

MYTH 2: Millennials Disrespect Authority

Many Millennials have authority issues. They come across as insubordinate or rude. It is a wide-spread rumor that Millennials are not fans of authority or any forms of traditional hierarchy.

Consider where the Millennial is coming from. This generation was raised by parents that opened proverbial doors for them, coaches that served as mentors, and guidance counselors that held their hand through school.

In fact, it was rather commonplace for parents of Millennials to call the coach to make sure their child gets put in the game or email the teacher to make sure the grades are on track. Instead of posting who made the school musical on a bulletin board, the directors had to first email parents to soften the blow. Heaven forbid any child being singled out when the cast list was posted.

Schools as a whole are adding more support and administration staff to keep up not only with the student but really more for their Helicopter Parents. During the school age years of nearly every previous generation, schools used to have one guidance counselor. Now, schools have one counselor for what seems like every letter of the alphabet.

According to the Bureau of Labor, in 2014 there were more than two-hundred and seventy-three thousand counselors working in public and private schools across the country. Do not get me wrong, caring for mental health is critical as is career coaching. My main point is that there has been a dramatic shift in culture. Counselors reported helping students cope with rising anxiety surrounding daily pressures and their image on social media.

During my time at Elon University, I was a Resident Assistant, better known as an RA. The role involved a number of things but at the core of it was making sure the campus was a safe livable space. There were eleven buildings in our area, each housing anywhere from thirty-two to seventy students.

By my fourth year at Elon, I was promoted to Resident Area Coordinator (RAC), which was one of the highest student-held positions on campus. You could call it the RA of the RAs but the reality was there was more desk work.

My office hours would involve working on the administrative side of residence life. But the most interesting part of the RAC job was answering the area phone. What was mind boggling to me was how many parents would call to check in on their child. The following are all based on true stories and are not exaggerated. Names have been changed.

Johnny's Mom
11:02 AM "Hi! I'm Johnny's mom! I texted him at 10:53 and haven't heard from, could you send someone to check on him."

"Thank you for calling," I replied. "I am sorry to hear that you cannot get a hold of your son Johnny. At 10:53 on what day did you last hear from Johnny?"

"This morning!" the frantic voice replied.

True story.

Taylor's Mom
"Do you have a laundry at Elon?"

"Yes Ma'am we do," I responded. "Every building is equipped with several washers and dryers per floor so students should always have access to clean their clothes."

A slight pause filled the line and the mother responded, "No I mean are you able to do laundry for my student. They never have had to do laundry before, and they do not know how to use your washer and dryer."

Yet again, true story. And it was not always mothers that called.

Time and time again, parents would call. Roommate troubles. Parents would call. If a student was locked out, parents would call. I mean it took more time for the student to text their parent and have their parent call the office than it would have taken for the student themselves to walk down to the office and get a new key. Now Elon has a high caliber of students and constantly outranks Ivy League institutions on many criteria, so this is not a poor reflection on the wonderful university that it is. Instead, it is a sad reality of the interactions parents have on behalf of their Millennial children.

In most of these cases, the Millennial child was between the ages of eighteen and twenty-two. That means the individual was fully capable of getting married, gambling, going to war, smoking, drinking...you name it. Yet, they texted their parents and had the parents call the school.

Even after college, some employers have told stories about Millennials bringing parents along on interviews or having a parent contact human resources to negotiate better benefits. While I personally have never had a parent intervene, I have on more than one occasion had a Millennial job candidate wait to accept a job until talking to their mom and dad.

Interacting with Millennials in the Workplace

Here is an exercise for you. Take off your manager hat for just a minute and put on your friend hat. Think about interactions that you have on a regular basis with your co-workers. Think about how they talk with you. Now picture that Millennial employee. Does that Millennial talk to you like they would talk to a peer? Chances are, that Millennial treats you as an equal while you view them as a subordinate.

Now, I am not saying this is right or how it should be. That said, it is important to remember that every adult and authority figure in a Millennial's life has been a friend. Millennials were raised to be confident, express their feelings, follow their passion and speak up — even if it is to senior management. Often this comes across as disrespectful and entitled.

Millennials grew up with a completely new set of rules that does not involve traditional authoritarian boundaries. So, when they seem insubordinate, they may not even realize they are breaking the hierarchical rules at all. Instead, Millennials are longing for your approval. Subconsciously, many in this generation feel that if they interact with you as they would a classmate, they will win your affection. That typical is the opposite reaction. Many Millennials that have been in the workforce for some time have matured and have overcome this childish instinct.

There are a number of ways that this disrespect rears its head. One common complaint is the fact that Millennials are glued to their phones. This is true. Many managers have shared their frustration that it is impossible to have a conversation without a Millennial turning to their cell phone.

Imagine a meeting in your office. You have a number of people around the table, including a few Millennials. As you are conversing and trying to move your business forward, something across the table catches your eye. The Millennial on their cell phone. You start to grow angry. Instead of being engaged in the current conversation this individual's face is illuminated by the bluish glow of their cell phone screen reflecting off their face. A common response is to, out of a place of frustration, tell everyone to turn off and put away their cell phones.

The reality is -- there could be a chance, and by no means am I saying that this is the case even most of the time -- that the Millennial could be checking up on a vocabulary word of business theory you just mentioned. There is a chance that they could be actively engaged in your conversation but by staring at their screen. Now, I am not making excuses for excessive technological usage and even addiction. A Millennial could just maybe be a more active listener than you think. They just do a poor job of showing it.

As independent thinkers, Millennials are being productive in the best way they know how, which might be multitasking while you are talking to them. This is not to excuse a Millennial's disconnected behavior. We will talk about strategies in a later chapter on how to combat technological distractions in the workplace. The important thing to note here is that even when a Millennial turns to their phone or devices, they may not always be disengaged.

For the most part, members of Generation X disliked their upbringing as latchkey kids. Many could not stand coming home to an empty home after school and waiting several hours for their career-driven parents to return home after a long day of work. When it came time for Gen Xers to have kids — the Millennials — they made sure they would never have to endure what they went through, leading to this overbearing and over involved style of parenting. For Millennials born to Boomers, a similar phenomenon occurred leading to entitlement. However, in this case, it was not an overinvolvement that fostered entitlement -- it was more of an over idealizing. Boomers wanted trophy children, a bragging right. They wanted children that added to their status and increased their clout.

Ironically, Millennial children of both Boomer and Gen Xer parents grew up being the focal point of the attention of their parents, but for two very different reasons. In both scenarios, the outcome was the same. This hyper-attention on children ultimately led to Millennials feeling the world revolved around them. Millennials have become the center of their parent's universe.

Nearly all of the adults in a Millennial's life have worked hard to make sure the members of this generation were always. In a world full of terror, wars and school shootings, parents, teachers and coaches naturally tried to provide a safe and friendly environment. In an effort to shelter the generation from the harsh realities of this broken world, authority figures often overcompensated by creating "safe places" and trying to make life a bit more approachable. Vernacular changed to be more inclusive -- salesmen became salespeople and freshmen back first years. Homosexuality transitioned from something that was shunned if found out to now celebrated when someone comes out.

Talking about sexual encounters with parents was taboo for Gen Xers and definitely for Boomers, but for Millennials, it was part of the coming of age. Parents no longer had to give the dreaded "talk" about the birds and the bees because media and accessibility to information educated Millennials. Instead, parents talked more openly with their children about sexual exploration.

While many archaic practices and verbiage needed an update to be relevant in modern society, these changes continued to solidify Millennial's desires, emotions and wants being at the center of the universe. This created an openness where Millennials are not afraid to speak their mind. To Boomers, this comes across as disrespect. To Gen X-ers this comes across as entitlement.

Because of the unique cultural shifts, protocols and unspoken rules do not going to fly with your Millennial staff members. The subtle societal rules that governed business meetings and human interactions do not apply to Millennials. If it is not engraved in stone tablets, it is optional. Instead, this young generation needs to work in environments with honest, open-door policies. Leaders that are approachable and friendly. Millennials are seasoned when it comes to self-expression. And yet, more often than not, they handle their expression in an immature manner. Closing off communication for letting a Millennial tell you "how they feel" about something is actually quite defeating.

Managing Through a Millennial's Negative Communication Style

A Millennial has undoubtedly busted down your door to tell you everything wrong in your organization. In that moment, they lacked tact. They wanted to share their feelings but more than likely stated their emotions as fact. Many leaders' gut reaction is to kick that ranting Millennial out of their office and often out to the curb.

Stop! You have a constant feedback loop and access to unprecedented workplace culture gossip. A Millennial is not good at keeping secrets. They've posted their entire life on the web for all to observe. Instead of shutting down these rants, help guide a Millennial to give productive criticism about your organization.

Take the threads of value woven throughout their soapbox of your organization is not inclusive and does not pay enough and instead help them realize that their insight is valuable if delivered in a more constructive way. Lean into the openness Millennials have and realize that the entitled and sometimes negative-seeming attitude is actual a window into your organization's health. You may be surprised what nuggets of wisdom you can gain from these tirades.

Millennials want to learn and be guided, not be told what to do. Use each of these conversations that make you boil up inside to coach a Millennial on how to deliver effective and actionable information. As a leader in your organization, you can help to shape their communication patterns into a great force for positive change in your company.

Nearly every Millennial wants to be a part of change. Use their emboldened gumption to your advantage. Inevitably, this will mean sitting through a frustrating rant or two. However, think about the great satisfaction of converting that seemingly emotionally charged information into a valuable resource for your organization. All the while, you can inspire Millennials to feel as if they are a change agent making a profound impact in your company. It is truly a win-win.

In general, because Millennials treat authority figures in their lives as mentors or equals, they do not conform to a traditional chain of command. Often, this generation refuses to follow traditional boundaries. In fact, they disagree with them entirely. To the average Millennial, there is nothing wrong with popping your head into the CEO's office just to chat, a CEO is just a person. Once again, social media is to thank. These networking platforms have allowed Millennials to interact with celebrities and politicians with a few swipes and movements of their thumbs. There is essentially no barrier to interacting with their favorite sitcom star and indie-musical artist. What is to make their boss or their boss's boss seem any different?

So how do you gain respect from this seemingly self-centered, respect-lacking generation? Through your actions. Part of a Millennial's complete disregard for corporate structure and positional hierarchy is because they do not respect titles. Titles are fake news. To many Millennials, those that have achieved some level of leadership in an organization clawed their way to get their and left a trail of bodies in their wake. To many Millennials, they heard stories of their parents playing the corporate game. They saw their parents get laid off. As a result of growing up around the cut-throat nature that previously existed in corporate America, Millennials feel that many that have risen to leadership are disingenuous.

Millennials often view top organizational leaders as hypocrites because they are unapproachable or cannot relate to the common person. Most of the time, these individuals operate behind the curtain — or behind the closed board room door. These higher ups are not as approachable as the celebrities on Instagram. Many Millennials feel as if the executives at the top are making exponentially more money (probably true) and do not work as hard as the poor entry-level Millennial.

To combat that, you must lead by example. Millennials will respect managers by their actions. Practice what you preach and you will have Millennials backing you all day long. For Millennials, respect is a two-way street because they see themselves as equal players.

If you have noticed yourself getting frustrated with the disrespectful nature of your Millennial employees, you are not alone. Instead of letting your frustration fuel your lack of confidence in this rising generation, focus on how you can tap into some of the new strengths.

A Millennial's confidence to barge into your office is now an open invitation for you to learn the rumblings of your organization. If played correctly, you can develop an ally with boots on the ground that can help open your eyes to different perspectives. Not if, but when they step out of lines and come across as disrespectful, entitled or negative, do not immediately shut them down. Speak in terms that relate to them. "Hey, I value your insight and perspective in our organization. You see things in a different way than I do. However, when you present information to me, it can come across as complaining or disrespectful which makes it difficult to hear the valuable information you are bringing to me that could help this organization. Could you bring concrete examples or stories as well as maybe your thoughts on how to address some of these opportunities?"

By having that conversation, you have just made yourself a hero. You are acknowledging a Millennial's concerns, letting them know that their insight is valuable and that their insight can help the greater organization. You are giving them concrete boundaries on how to communicate more effectively, you are coaching them to deliver information to leadership properly and you are leaving the door open.

Most importantly, you have also established trust. Chances are, a Millennial is still going to break the chain of command and say something totally inappropriate and disrespectful. However, you have now coached them to be better. And Millennials eat that up. Try to see your Millennial team members as independent thinkers who are trying to engage, be curious, express themselves and make a contribution in the office.

Believe it or not, as rudimentary as a conversation like that may seem, chances are you will only need to have that once and that will minimize your problems in the disrespect area. Unfortunately, many leaders are too proud or get too heated to have these conversations. As a result, the leader becomes more frustrated and the Millennial becomes dissatisfied with their workplace and leaves. The problem is solved...until you hire your next Millennial.

TRUTH: Every adult in a Millennial's life has been a friend, a coach, or a mentor, but not a boss. Elders are seen as equals, not as superiors. Respect is earned, not automatic because of age or corporate hierarchy. It is very likely Millennials have no idea how their actions may come across to you or other adults in their life.

MYTH 3: Millennials Are Lazy

Check your email. I bet in the last twenty-four hours, if you manage more than a dozen Millennials, you have received an email from a Millennial about better work-life balance. It may be an email from last night at 4:59 PM and a Millennial responded,

"I'll work on that tomorrow -- Sent from my iPhone."

The team member was already out the door and responding to you on their mobile device. If you manage Millennials at all, I would wager that at some point that younger employee has asked you for flexible time, unlimited paid time off or a better work-life balance. Do not fear. You are not alone.

There are several reasons for this, but in general, Millennials work to live, they do not live to work. Meaning, work for Millennials is a form of survival. It digs them out of their student debt and pays for their organic avocado toast delivery. Work is just an annoyance that occupies, on a bad week, up to forty hours of their time. For more mature generations, this notion can be exceedingly frustrating.

The Infamous Work-Life Balance Conundrum

So why do Millennials care so much about work-life balance? While it might be easy to assume this plea for flexibility is due to the fact that a Millennial is lazy or they just do not want to work, this reaction is a reflect. Think about their childhood. Growing up, Millennials had parents who were at the office quite a bit. That said, parents would often come to support sporting events and concerts. The notion of work-life balance does not stem from a lack of parental support. On the contrary, Millennials were so involved and structured in different extracurriculars that their childhood of playing in the creek and riding bikes around the block was stunted. Because of the parents' work schedules, Millennials were thrust into these extra programs as a form of childcare. Being bound to a strict scheduled subconsciously robbed many Millennials of the freedom of being a care-free child.

When the school bell rang at 3:00 PM, Millennials were just getting started. Millennials understand the go-go-go lifestyle better than any previous generation. From extracurriculars to homework, Millennials grew up very quickly. Between waiting for the bus, classroom time and after school activities, it was not uncommon for Millennials to spend as many as nine to ten hours on average away from home Monday through Friday. That would be the equivalent of almost a fifty-hour work week. Then add games to some of those evenings, the events of their siblings and then weekend activities. As elementary schoolers, this generation was working seven days a week. That does not even include homework time. So to say that Millennials are lazy could in fact be one of the biggest myths about the generation of all time.

Millennials know busyness. They know hard work. They understand efficiency and how to just get things done. Yet, when it comes to their job, 10:00 AM to 3:00 PM seems good enough for them.

This lackadaisical work attitude is one of the greatest conundrums for employers of Millennials. If Millennials truly have the capacity to work long hours, how then can you get a Millennial to work harder?

One of the key things to measure is not hours worked. For Boomers, this is heresy. No matter your organization, it is far more important to measure output than it is to measure hours worked. Output has two key measures: quantity and quality. Most Boomers would prefer quantity over quality. To Boomers, the more hours one works, the better company-person that individual is. With a Millennial, you often will get the bare minimum work requested completed in as few work hours as humanly possible. For Gen X-ers, quality was more important. Getting the work done right away and all the way was key. When a member of Generation X signed off for the night, they wanted to rest assured that their work was completed, and they would not have to hear from their boss again until the next morning. This generation typically produced quality work so that there were no urgent fires that would have to be put out after work hours. However, if there was a need, most Gen X-ers would step up to the plate, even after hours.

Where does that leave Millennials? Millennials know efficiency. They also know technology. It is also important to note that Millennials do exactly what they are told -- no more and no less. If you tell a Millennial to jump, they will have their phone out calculating the fastest way to jump before you finish your instructions. They will jump, not caring how high, and expect your doting praise for a job well done.

If you had hoped for the Millennial to figure out a way to jump across the Grand Canyon, then you should have said so. Giving the Millennial a clear goal will set that Millennial on a mission to complete it. They will first pull out their phone and Google, "The shortest part of the Grand Canyon." The result will turn up the result: "The narrowest point of the Grand Canyon is in Marble Canyon and is 600 feet wide. The widest point of the Grand Canyon is 18 miles wide." Great, their goal is now 600 feet. You were hoping for the eighteen miles.

An efficient childhood, crammed full of activities combined with the accessibility of technology, how-to videos and online resources has caused Millennials to work at warp speed. They will often choose the path of least resistance, hoping for a reward at the end of their task.

While a Millennial will work quickly, they often complete tasks with a level of quality. They want their supervisor's admiration and praise. More often than not, Millennials do produce quality of work. But again, it will be the bare minimum.

When motivating a Millennial to complete a task, give them crystal clear instructions. If you have a clear idea of what is that you are hoping to receive, tell them. Without clear direction, a Millennial will have great pride in completing a project with decent quality in record speed. When they turn it over to their manager, if the manager is dissatisfied at all, a Millennial is often defeated. In their mind, they did exactly what was asked of them and they did it well.

As you assign tasks to your team members of the Millennial generation, be sure to include expectations. They grew up in the day of rubrics. A rubric is an educational grading tool that provides a somewhat objective grading method in subjective projects. There are usually several criteria each with bucketed results. Try assigning tasks in a similar fashion.

Take a project and break it down into expectations. Let them know you will be exceedingly pleased if the project is completed by a given date at a certain time and has X, Y and Z components. Then give them the downside scenario too. Explain what will not meet your expectations.

Using this management technique, you will be astounded how your results change. A Millennial will almost always complete a task to the level and at the speed in which they are instructed as long as it is feasible and reasonable. They will find much more satisfaction knowing your expectations along the way. Ambiguous instructions are a Millennial's worst nightmare. They will work hard to please you, but if they are working on an initiative and do not know how to please you, they will spin their tires and grow frustrated.

It is important to remember that if you do use a rubric-type approach, you need to stick to your assignment. Do not change requirements or time frames if at all possible. Obviously, business situations arise that require pivoting. In that case, communicate clearly the change and the new expectations. Communication, as in all relationships, is key.

Once a project is complete, be sure to specifically thank a Millennial for completing the task to your requirements if they have done so. If they have not met the requirements you set out, let them know and explain how you would have preferred to see the final product delivered. Often, as long as you are not adding requirements to a project after delivery, a Millennial will take the feedback well. Millennials actually thrive with constructive feedback.

Millennials are Aspiring World Travelers

There is another primary reason that causes Millennials to give off that lazy vibe. It stems from peer pressure. Millennials do often expect flexible work schedules. They believe in this idea of remote work. Their friends are virtual, so they think their job should be too. There are many times where a Millennial completes their work exceptionally fast due to their inherent inclination towards technology and desire for efficiency. What do Millennials do once they have completed an assignment? They reward themselves with a social media break.

They pull out their phone, which was more than likely already on their desk, and start thumbing through Instagram. Their best friend just landed in Maui and their college roommate is riding a camel in Egypt. That person that they have never met but is friend of a friend's aunt's dog is currently scuba diving in the Greater Barrier Reef. Not one of their friends posted a picture of their office.

Scrolling through social media often gives off an appearance that no one has a traditional desk job anymore. Many Millennials' news feeds are filled with their friends who are off making money as a blogger, an influencer or a travel writer… whatever it is, it beats sitting in a cubicle all day. You have heard of the starving artist, right? Well now this generation has the starving influencer. They are typically making little cash for their social posts, but the positive side is they are getting thousands of dollars in free flights, hotels, meals and experiences.

A few years ago, I was consulting with a software start-up. The executive that hired me was a tweener between being a Baby Boomer and member of Generation X. He was right on the line. There were several hundred people in this location of the company's offices. The majority were fresh out of college. As this executive toured me around the facility, he intentionally walked me up and down the aisles of cubicles — most tours you stay in the main corridors.

Now that is always a loaded question because there were many things I felt like commenting on, but I was not sure what he was getting at. "What specifically are you referring to?" I replied, hoping to get a clearer idea of what type of feedback he was vying for so early in our consulting agreement.

"The people. What did you notice about our team and how they interacted with me as well as others?"

Immediately I knew what he was getting at. Boldly I said, "No working."

You see, out of the hundreds of people in that office, many were smack dab in the middle of the Millennial generation. Walking around, I saw people playing games on their computers, texting, scrolling through social media on their phones, streaming Netflix on their tablets and the list goes on.

To get to the point, after several months of consulting with them, the solution was rather simple. They had entirely too many team members for the workload. The team members were bored. There were underlying leadership and management issues as well. Most of which could have been solved with the ideas in this book. The scenario is not all too uncommon anymore. Millennials work much more quickly and have a high capacity to complete a lot of work in a short period of time. But, the second the supply of new projects runs out, you have lost a Millennial's attention.

Millennials Leave at 3:00 PM

As Millennials entered the workforce, employers started to realize trends where young team members had the notion that they could leave work at three in the afternoon. Call it entitled, call it lazy -- at the end of the day it is a problem. It appears as if Millennials are not as productive as prior generations.

The productivity of most Millennials, if measured by the amount of quality output in a given time window, is likely higher than that of the preceding generations. The truth is, Millennials are not lazy, they probably just finished their work early. This generation grew up with the internet and with technology. Since Millennials, as a whole, are so tech-savvy, most can complete a task faster than the average employee. Millennials try to do things in the most efficient way possible, which is why they order their lunch and have it delivered and send out their laundry. It is not lazy as much as it is efficient.

But here's the rub. When you get down to it, if an organization measured a Millennial's productivity of the most basic work tasks, it would surpass that of the Gen X-ers and run circles around the Baby Boomers. However, there is a fundamental difference. Millennials will stop at the bare minimum. When they are done, they will want to leave early. In their eyes, they have completed the task set out for them and it is time to move on.

Generation X is the opposite. Once a task is completed, most Gen X-ers will look for opportunities to take initiative and go above and beyond to fill the remainder of their workday. They were used to this. Coming home from school without parents being home taught them how to occupy time. Millennials are more concerned about getting work done so they can Occupy Wall Street.

Baby Boomers are more inclined to burn their time by doing a task more slowly and appearing to be productive when in reality, they are just biding their time to be the last person to leave the building. Baby Boomers also rarely multi-task. That is why cell phones in meetings are often frowned upon by Boomers. They complete tasks very sequentially.

On the other hand, Millennials are used to doing things on the go. Multi-tasking, such as answering emails and making calls while running errands and walking their dog is normal. With this mindset, Millennials do not see a need to sit at a desk for work they could do while tackling their personal to-do lists. To this generation, life is all intertwined.

So when a Millennial leaves at three in the afternoon, they may actually be willing to be on call until later in the evening. If they like their work and respect their employer, it is not out of place for a Millennial to email in bed as they fall asleep and send a Slack message first thing in the morning when they wake up.

Conversely, if the Millennial is not a fan of his or her job and does not feel appreciated nor like they are an active contributor to the larger organization, chances are, they will be checked out two hours before five and will not be checked back into work until they are on their third macchiato of the morning.

So, while it might seem like this generation is lazy, they are actually adding more hours to their work week than previous generations. More than one third of Millennials reported working every day while on vacation because they liked feeling needed or they wanted to impress their boss. Remember, Millennials are people pleasers. The other two thirds of

Millennials probably did not feel satisfied in their job nor feel like they were making a difference.

Working Hard for the World

Making a difference is a big deal to this generation. Many Millennials are looking to find a way to make a living while also embracing their passions. They want a job with purpose. Millennials will go above and beyond to fight for a cause they care about. More than nearly any prior generation, Millennials are passionate about people and the planet.

With media making the world so interconnected, Millennials truly are global citizens. Further, with air travel more affordable and convenient than it has ever been, eighty-two percent of Millennials travel outside of their state for pleasure every year. Ninety-seven percent of those will post an average of two to three posts per day of their travels on social media. To put that in perspective, only about twelve percent of Gen X-ers travel out of state for pleasure each year.

Millennials have seen the world and continue to see the world both in person and through media. This global awareness increases Millennials likelihood to support not-for-profit organizations and their missions.

Outside of their work, seventy-three percent of Millennials will volunteer for nonprofits. Most previous generations average only about thirty percent participation in philanthropic activities. Millennials lead the way in championing altruistic activities. In addition to volunteering, fifty-two percent of Millennials donate to a nonprofit at least once monthly. That level of benevolence is unprecedented.

Now, the big difference between Millennials and other generations is that they are going to give a whole lot less money. They still put a high priority on their Netflix, Stitch Fix and Home Chef memberships. But they are going to give monthly, and that's a substantial commitment.

Finally, eighty percent of Millennials feel pulled to fight for a cause over a nonprofit organization. A nonprofit is a group of people working toward a cause, but Millennials see them as an entity of people in suits that are sitting behind desks making decisions for them instead of a cohort of people that is moving in the same direction. They are more connected to causes over nonprofits, because they view institutions negatively. A cause is a *friend*.

Millennials have this distrust for people that are going to spend their money. They would rather be unified with their community because they're used to groups and friends and their friends are going to move in the same direction. This is why they're much more likely to band together behind a cause.

Climate change is one of the many causes that Millennials want to combat because they've seen all of the related issues around the world. They have so much real-time exposure to global news.

Millennials are usually well-rounded individuals, as they are versed in the arts, science, music, and sports. Because of this, they often have a better understanding of the world — probably more than any other generation. Arguably, Millennials have had more access to information than any other generation in the past. Much of that information is then retained.

Regardless, Millennials want to believe in something bigger than themselves. So, if the team and the winningest sport thing is bigger than themselves, that's what they want to do. If their following on social media makes them bigger than they actually are, that's what they want to be a part of.

If they want to go see the world change on the other side of the planet because they have pen pals that are there now… Wait, they don't even know what a pen pal is because they've never picked up a pen in their life! Just kidding.

Millennials will always believe in — and want to be a part of — something bigger than themselves. How do you take that back to your office?

It's important to keep in mind that they are not self-starters because they like structure — not the kind of structure to eliminate their creativity but structure so they have a clear plan and course of action. Start by giving them the goal of something you're trying to accomplish.

Manage with Metrics, Motivate with Goals

Millennials are the most goal-driven and metric-driven generation of all time. Their entire life has been numbers. How many followers you have on social media, how many minutes you spend in front of a screen, how many friends you have on your video game channel, the list goes on.

Take a numerical goal but add a twist to it and tell the Millennial how that goal will make an impact for the greater good. For example, instead of saying, "Our company has to make $1.2 million this year," say, "Our goal is to impact (this number of) customers and (this many) lives."

The Millennial will instantly be on board!

You have to change your spin on it, because now, it's not appealing when it's about numbers and money, which only benefits company owners. Even though they understand numbers better than anyone else, Millennials would rather talk about how they're helping to make a positive impact instead.

Yes, you can set metrics and numbers and goals and say, "We want to hit this number," but you can also say, "Hey, we want to improve this many people's lives so they can reach their goals and that will equal (this much) money."

If your company does any work for a cause, or you have considered it, this could be your chance to engage those employees. Get them involved in the event or a day or service. This will give them a chance to get out of the office, get behind a cause and have an experience they can take pictures of to share with their virtual friends.

Now you're putting something in front of them that they are excited about — this is something that they can get behind, this big goal, something bigger than themselves, and that's really all that they want to do.

So, what ultimately matters here is that Millennials care a lot about their work environment and what it's like. Millennials need constructive feedback and they want structure.

Structured Freedom

A term I love to use is *structured freedom*. It is how Millennials have been raised. The best way to explain this concept is a sports field or arena.

Think about soccer. There are clear boundaries on the field from the sidelines to the goal lines. There are clear roles for the players, managers and coaches. Each team has an objective that is identified.

Day in and day out, a team will practice under the direction of a coach. The coach will instruct the team how to win the game. They will rehearse defense and offense strategies. Each player will know their specific role on the field. They know the rules of the field, where they can go and where they cannot go. They know where the ball must be to be in bounds and they know where the ball must end up to win. Each player knows his or her responsibility as well as a set of guidelines and things that they are not allowed to do. If the slide tackle, they know they could be carded. If they kick the ball out of bounds, they know the other team will get to toss it in. If they are offsides, they know there could be a penalty kick.

Every single guideline, boundary and rule is crystal clear. The end goal is absolute. It is always in the same place.

All of those items lend themselves to structure. Then you have the freedom portion. Once the whistle blows during the game, the clock starts. With the clock running, the ball can go in any direction and everyone on the field can do just about whatever they want as long as it is within the structured boundaries, guidelines and rules.

The best players, the ones who receive the MVP trophy, are the ones who think fast and think creatively. They can size up the competition and figure out how to get the ball into the opposing team's goal to score a point. They know how to win.

Millennials love structured freedom. They love to know how to win and they love to know what they are and are not allowed to do to reach that goal. Further, Millennials love working with a team and love the guidance and supervision of a coach.

Being competitively natured, they will inevitably bend a rule and the ref will call them on it. More often than not, they will take the penalty well and get back in the game and run towards winning.

Creating structured freedom environments is a win-win management technique for Millennials. Millennials have a clear direction and know expectations. Simultaneously, they are granted some autonomy and freedom as long as the play within the lines.

A manager can sit back and watch how the Millennial dribbles the ball down the field towards the goal. Sometimes, there may need to be some correcting, but usually, Millennials can complete a task entirely on their own if the expectations were clearly communicated.

Millennials are not as lazy as many think. Instead, they just need to clear boundaries and the freedom to take the ball down the field and kick it into the goal.

TRUTH: Millennials want to do everything as efficiently as possible. So, while they may appear lazy when they're having food delivered and sending out their weekly laundry, they are getting more work done than the generations before them did. Millennials are looking for ways to make a living while exercising their passions. They want a job with purpose, and they will rally for the greater good.

MYTH 4: Millennials Are Disloyal And Non-Committal

Most Millennials are willing to make a commitment if they know what is in it for them. Aren't we all like that to some extent? In general, sixteen months is the average tenure for a Millennial. The good news is that number is increasing, the bad news is this generation will likely hold three to five jobs before they are thirty.

Millennials are thinking, "If I'm going to work for you for a year, what is in it for me?" Sometimes, they will even be bold enough to ask that question. What are they *really* asking? They simply want to know how they will be in a better place, one year from now as a result of working with your organization. Will you change their lifestyle?

Up until the start of their career, everything in a Millennial's life has been scripted or planned for them. For example, if they are playing baseball, they know there is practice before the season, then they will have the actual games. If their team played well, they know there will be layoffs and then the mini-little-league World Series.

That roadmap is a schedule they can follow. They are willing to commit to long hours of practice when it is cold outside and everything else if they see the clear path to the finish line.

The disloyal and non-committal label typically is applied by previous generations who have a radically different perspective of loyalty. Baby Boomers are all about staying loyal to the company. Remember, Boomers are often more about quantity over quality. They are likely to walk into a job on day one and be thinking about the next twenty-five years between that moment and their retirement. A member of Generation X will walk in on day one planning to stay but is often open to another opportunity if it fits their current life stage better. However, they are less likely to job hop unless head-hunted.

Conversely, a Millennial walks in on day one longing for a clear path to retirement. They need step-by-step guidelines as to when they are getting a raise, when they will be able to afford a house, when they feel they have enough cash flow to start a family and so on. Often, if a Millennial does not get clear answers to some of these life stages from their offer letter, a Millennial is already thinking of their next job before they report to work on the first day at your company.

Many previous generations do not understand why a Millennial needs this planned career path. It comes across as disloyal.

Millennials are giving off this attitude of, "Show me where I'm going to be in the future, and I'll start today and I'll get there as fast as humanly possible."

Harnessing a Millennial's Drive and Ambition

This drive and ambition is something that should be harnessed and guided. Many managers are afraid of this attitude because it sends up red flags that the Millennial is already on their way out before they even start. In reality, Millennials want to be trained and coached because all that have had their whole life is adult authority figures-turned-friends. These friend/coach/mentors literally have helped guide Millennials through every step of their life. This generation has had to figure out very few things on their own. When a mentor was not there to walk them through something, Google was.

Millennials are not afraid to change positions, jobs or even make a career switch if it means it will put them a step closer to their goals. If you promise a Millennial the moon and you do not deliver, they are looking for someone else to deliver the moon to them.

Research shows that more than forty percent of Millennials plan to leave their jobs within two years and less than thirty percent of them want to be in the same job for more than five years. *Planning* is the key word in that statistic. Nearly half plan to their jobs but a significant number more will spontaneously leave in less time than two years. Leading causes are simply an employer failing to follow through on promises.

According to the Bureau of Labor, statistics show that the average job tenure for Americans in their twenties and thirties was almost the same in the eighties as it is today. In 1983, the average number of years spent at a job was three, compared to two years and ten months in 2018.

However, the reasoning for switching jobs is often much different today than what it was in the eighties. Millennials have a much different mentality than those of the Baby Boomers and Gen X-ers. In fact, Millennials are three times more likely to switch jobs and to relocate than any previous generation. Furthermore, seventy-five percent of Millennials say job-hopping has actually helped them advance in their careers.

Overcoming Millennial's Aversion to Grunt Work

Have you ever felt like Millennials do not want to do grunt work? Or maybe that they are unwilling to do the little things? The reality is that a Millennial do not see the *purpose* of grunt work. Millennials will almost work towards a bigger goal. They just need to see it. This generation has their eye on the finish line. They are classically condition to know once they cross the finish line, a reward awaits them.

If you say, "Can you clean up the front lobby and straighten up your workstation?" A Millennial is going to think, "That is ridiculously boring and beneath me." In other words, the grunt work was not in the plan. This is yet another interaction that earns the Millennial the disloyal, disrespectful and lazy title.

However, if you frame menial tasks differently, Millennials are more likely to get on board. First of all, acknowledge that a task is outside of their job description. Then tie the task back to the overall goal and mission of the company. For example, you could say "I have a favor to ask of you. We have a really big client coming in that could really provide new opportunities for the company, do you have time to help straighten up your workspace and our entry area to give them the best first impression possible?"

By repositioning the chore, you can easily gain a Millennial's buy in. All of a sudden, the task is about making other people happier. You are letting the team members be a part of something bigger than themselves. Now the task is not about sweeping floors.

Millennials are always looking for new experiences. They thrive on short-term goals with visible results. Millennials love structure as long as the structure is ultimately going to make things better for the greater good. This generation also loves numbers and data. As we looked at earlier, their metrics-driven mindsets are all thanks to social media.

It is likely no surprise, but a recent workplace study revealed that forty percent of Millennial employees feel unfulfilled and unengaged in their current jobs. This is likely the reason that about the same number have already contemplated leaving their job within two years of starting. The primary source for this discontentment stems from a place of feeling like promises went unfilled. Many Millennials are promised growth opportunities during the hiring process. On day one, many milestones are set out that seem like exciting opportunities.

Most of these are misleading management tactics that leave a Millennial feeling like they were handed a stack of fake news about their new job. Nearly eight out of every ten Millennials confess looking on job boards for new jobs at least several times a year — even if they are not planning to apply. Millennials are information gatherers and want to make sure that they are in the best place for them to move forward and thrive.

Millennials, being very emotionally driven, will also jump at another opportunity the second a major career promise is broken by their current employer. I cannot begin to tell you the number of exit interviews I have had with Millennials. In nearly every situation, when I would dig deep, the Millennial would point back to something during their hiring process that they were led to believe about their career trajectory. Their chief reason for leaving, in my experience, is their manager's failed ability to deliver on promises. This causes a Millennial to feel betrayed and lied to and as a result, whether vindictive or just simply self-serving, a Millennial quits.

Millennials Would Prefer to Stay in Their Current Job If....

The encouraging truth is that ninety percent of Millennials want to grow their career within their current company. Eighty percent said further training and development opportunities at work would keep them from leaving their current position. Millennials are craving growth opportunities.

Further, they demand corporate accountability. If they are promised something, they feel entitled to receive what was offered to them. As we discussed several pages ago, you can outline hard criteria and milestones several years into the future for a Millennial. That will not scare them off. They want clear strategies to move throughout an organization. Do not be surprised when a Millennial completes all of the milestones in an abbreviated timeline and comes knocking at your door for their reward. If their reward is not ready, they are going to start looking elsewhere.

A great way to retain Millennials is to various career advancement pathways. To provide these growth opportunities, managers must help Millennials identify ways to develop new skills. These opportunities could be anything from providing them with new tasks, job-shadowing someone else in the office, or maybe they plan a new company event. Millennials love special projects that they can own. It breaks up the monotony of their day and allows them to develop pride over a project or event for your company. Plus, in these types of roles, Millennials get to work cross-functionally with different team members in the organization. This creates a physical social network that anchors a Millennial to your company. Bonus points if you can think of ways to get the Millennial out of the office setting and really provide a one-of-a-kind experience for them.

Millennials are also appreciative of any opportunity that puts their skills in front of a superior. A Millennial always loves to impress their boss, but their boss's boss is an even bigger incentive. If your office has a management committee or informal events with higher management, allowing a Millennial to present will give them a tweet-worthy corporate experience. This also makes a Millennial feel like they are more connected to the organization at all levels further solidifying their loyalty.

Millennials are especially motivated by dynamic, cross-functional positions. They also seek jobs that allow them to be in contact with and learn from interesting people, interacting with other professionals and teams. For this reason, their career paths should offer a wide range of experiences and not just vertical promotions. These organization-wide interactions provide satisfaction to many Millennials. Twenty percent of Millennials say that finding a job that is more fulfilling would be the biggest factor in the decision to leave their current job.

Providing Feedback

If a Millennial does not know how they are doing, they are going to assume the worst. If they think you, as their manager, may fire them, they are going to remove themselves from your organization before that happens.

A great way to overcome the questioning and insecure mind of a Millennials it to provide feedback. Make it a habit to provide feedback more than once per year. Annual reviews are a thing of the past. As many as seventy-two percent of Millennials who receive regular feedback from management report feeling more fulfilled and satisfied at work.

This feedback does not need to be in a formal setting all of the time. Nor should it be. Remember, Millennials want acknowledgment and if they are not doing a good job, they want to know so they can fix it. Again, if criticism is presented correctly, Millennials will work diligently to improve. You do not want to wait a year to deliver feedback. Chances are, if you wait that long, a Millennial already has one foot out the door.

Millennials are often motivated by different things. Paid time off, flex time, travel perks and other benefits may seem absurd to previous generations. At the core, it is important to remember that Millennials are big dreamers with lofty goals. The big goal underpinning most of a Millennial's actions are a comfortable, flexible, and carefree lifestyle. Yes, that is idealistic, but that is the desire of many Millennial's hearts. Contrary to previous generations, Millennials are not necessarily enticed by job titles or even salaries. Money of course is a positive perk, but if you go back to the first chapter in this section, you will recall money is not the chief motivating factor. Simply put, Millennials want to be in places where they will have the most impact.

Millennials are focused on purpose, and if a job does not align with that purpose, they will find their way to the door. One company I was consulting with focused on designing innovative tools to streamline workplace efficiency. Their mission (and I'll summarize to protect the company's identity) was to create innovative solutions to make people's lives easier and happier. It was written in a much pithier and repeatable way and was plastered all over the hallways and meeting rooms of this company's corporate office. The company continually won awards and had virtually no voluntary turn over.

New leadership rolled in and within months, key team members started leaving and that trickled through the organization. A company that used to have stacks of resumes pouring in had a dried-up talent pool. Internal referrals for new hires ceased to exist. Great team members that had been there far beyond the average tenure for their age cohort were leaving. In a few interviews I conducted with team members on behalf of this company, I quickly learned that the team had perceived a shift in the company's core values. While the uplifting mantra was still lining the halls and engraved on plaques, the new leadership strayed away from running the business according to the core mission.

The Millennials were the first to jump ship, but it led a chain reaction throughout the organization. If Millennials feel betrayed by leadership or feel that leadership is not leading a business that is guided by core principles, Millennials are quick to exit. This turnover can cause fear in other generations too. Often, if there is a mass exodus, Gen X-ers will start to be open to new opportunities as well.

It is critical for leadership in an organization to stay true to the core values and mission set out. There are certainly times where values may be updated or enhanced, but it is crucial that those changes are clearly and carefully communicated with the organization. If a Millennial perceives that the talking heads do not practice what they preach, Millennials are out.

Businesses are often trying to figure out new ways to keep their Millennial employees by piling on office perks, including snacks and vacation days. These help but are often not at the core of a Millennial's dissatisfaction and lack of loyalty and commitment.

As a brief aside, there is often a myth surrounding Millennials that they have more than one job. The truth is, eighty-eight percent prefer the simplicity of having a single full-time job than having multiple part-time jobs. However, as many as fifty percent work a gig-job like Uber or Upwork. Many times, this is to break up the monotony of a mundane job or to earn extra cash for a lavish vacation. Their desire to work outside of their day-job proves they are not lazy. Often, if they are working on their side hustle during work hours it is because their day job does not keep them busy enough.

Millennials are not necessarily lazy. They just do exactly what you tell them to do and will likely not do anything extra. To combat this, create tangible goals for your Millennial team members. They measure their work by the end-result — what they have achieved — not the number of hours logged, organizational charts, scheduled breaks or strict dress codes. Give them concrete goals by which they can gauge their own performance. They will be their own harshest critic. Just like the Grand Canyon example earlier, if you tell them to jump, they will find the easiest path to reach the goal. This comes across as lazy. In reality, it is working smarter not harder. Providing crystal clear expectations will turn your Millennial workforce into a powerhouse.

TRUTH: Millennials are looking to conquer their career paths and they're willing to go wherever that leads them. The stigma surrounding job-hopping is fading fast and many Millennials say their career moves have helped them advance. To retain Millennials, companies will have to provide regular feedback, unique growth opportunities and career planning.

MYTH 5: Millennials Are Anti-Social

Nearly a decade ago, I was sitting in a small coffee shop with some of my best friends from college. The shop had previously been a bank and the vault was now a prevalent part of the aesthetic. For whatever reason, we decided to spend our time sipping our house roasts and discussing the future of our generation in America. What else are you going to chat about when catching up with your friends?

We were discussing how all of our friends from college were moving into cities. Some moved to New York, Chicago and Los Angeles. However, the majority were moving to what I would consider tier two cities—Austin, Durham, Nashville, Charlottesville and so on. We were surmising that the large majority of our friends were moving to these second-tier cities because they wanted to have the amenities of a big city without the financial burden.

Where I live now is a perfect example. My wife and I built a house in downtown Durham, North Carolina. The city only has a couple hundred thousand people, is not as expensive as Boston or Chicago yet has everything we could ever want. The city is home to one of the top five theaters in the nation where Broadway tours play. We a Triple A baseball team, the Durham Bulls and are next to Duke and University of North Carolina at Chapel Hill should we want a college-ball fix. The food and nightlife scene are moderate and all we need. We are next to an airport that has countless direct flights to anywhere we would ever want to go. We get all of these luxuries without the ridiculous traffic and costs associated with the top ten cities.

There are mixed messages surrounding the Millennial myth that dubs the generation as anti-social. Some people say Millennials are anti-social and they only prefer the online world, while others say they are actually so social that they are unable to pull themselves offline.

Think back to the time when Millennials were growing up. Instead of going outside to ride bikes or play with neighbor kids, they stayed in their rooms and logged onto the internet to chat or hovered over gaming consoles.

Because of this, this generation often does not regard face-to-face interaction with the same level of importance as members of previous generations. Instead, virtual communication, to many Millennials, is an appropriate form of conversing and building relationships.

Communicating on a smartphone or another digital device requires much less of an emotional investment, and in a way, it is impersonal. That said, Millennials do nearly everything online. Aside from social media, they attend classes and webinars online, they watch YouTube videos and stream shows. They even date and meet new friends from phone apps.

Life online allows them to send messages at all hours and they can connect with people who are anywhere in the world at any time. This generation never bought calling cards to contact their pen pal in Hong Kong. In fact, many Millennials never had a pen pal. If they did have an international friend, it was usually a keyboard pal.

Virtual Connectivity Can Cause Physical Dysconnectivity

The unlimited connectivity made the world a small place for Millennials. Being plugged in to the internet also meant that life online never stopped. To this day, for Millennials, it never stops. Even when members of this generation are logged off, they are psychologically still plugged in... Enter FoMO.

FoMO is real. You may be familiar with the phrase FoMO or you may be a victim of it. The trendy phrase stands for **F**ear **o**f **M**issing **O**ut. Millennials totally embrace and live by this mantra whether or not they know it. Experimental psychologist, Andrew Przybylski, has given FoMO a more formal definition: "pervasive apprehension that others might be having rewarding experiences from which one is absent." But PATOMBHREFWOIA does not have the same ring.

In fact, research shows that Millennials are tired of being constantly connected, but they attribute FoMO as an obstacle to taking digital-free breaks and vacations. As far as work goes, there is also FoBO — **F**ear **of B**etter **O**ptions. A report from LinkedIn shows FoBO as one of the top workplace challenges people face today, with sixty-eight percent of workers admitting to having it. The majority of that sixty-eight percent, as you may have guessed, is the Millennial generation.

FoBO has impacted me over the years. Both as an employee but also as an employer. In fact, one of the best examples I have is one of my best hires of all time — we will call them Charlie. Charlie was one of the highest producing, team-spirited, company people I had ever hired. Every goal set for Charlie was quickly surpassed — and Charlie is a Millennial believe it or not. As I exited this particular role, I was devastated to leave this team member behind. Unfortunately, my new opportunity did not have a role for Charlie's skillset.

Shortly after I had left, Charlie called expressing that they were not happy at their current situation, so they looked at several other companies. The reason Charlie called was for advice. This individual had received several incredible offers for more pay and better benefits. Simultaneously, their current work environment was deteriorating. It was a perfect time to move on.

After pitching in my two cents, I was fairly confident I knew which of the opportunities Charlie would take. Several weeks later, I received another phone call. Charlie informed me that they had declined all of the offers because there still could be one better.

This notion is preposterous but not uncommon for a Millennial. Like Charlie, many Millennials frequently apply for other jobs.

As a result, almost two years later, they are still at the same exact company; they have not moved at all. When trying to recruit a Millennial, it is important to encourage them and let them know that you are offering the best opportunity.

In a single minute in 2019, nearly two-hundred million emails, forty-two million WhatsApp messages, and eighteen million text messages are sent out. In that same time period, nearly five million YouTube videos are watched, five million gifs are viewed, one million Tindr photos are swiped, one million Facebook logins, nearly four million Google searches and half-a-million mobile app downloads happen. Millennials are always online — that's where their lives are!

The thing about that is, though, that Millennials have built this natural ability to build their image and a brand based on their personal experiences. This makes them really useful when it comes to marketing and communication, which is great. But it also has its downsides.

Studies show that thirty percent of this generation always or often feel lonely and twenty-two percent of them said they have no friends. Many experts point their fingers at social media for this, saying it's causing Millennials to miss out on valuable, in-person interactions. Because this group has created such perfect, curated images of themselves online, they are unable to make genuine connections with others.

Others say the loneliness could be a result of today's pressures, whether from work, society, the economy, or trying to start a family.

At the office, you may consider identifying Millennials employees that really excel at this and turn them into brand ambassadors. This would be a good way for the company to utilize their skills, but also for Millennials to be online while at work.

Millennials understand the importance of connecting to customers all over the world and they have the ability to create emotional connections through social media content. With small amounts of content, they can reach huge audiences — tap into this!

Your Millennial employees likely also have several personal connections that they can use to build a strong community. Because of their life online, Millennials can easily discern who their supporters are, and they are not afraid to ask them for help when they truly need it.

TRUTH: Millennials have mostly grown up online, and that includes making friends, growing relationships and even dating in digital spaces. They are comfortable living life online, and most of them are aware of how much screen time they've had each week. Some Millennials express a want to take breaks from digital life, but that's where everything is.

MYTH 6: Millennials Only Work At Trendy Companies

Millennials care about their work environment. If they are required to be somewhere all day, five days a week, they want their office to be trendy. Though that may be less of a grown-up version of Chuck E. Cheese than you are thinking.

For the large majority of my working life, I was under the assumption that offices I worked with and consulted for needed hoverboards and drones to attract Millennials. It seemed that more than fringe benefits, the in-office amenities would attract and retain the best talent. Turns out, that is not necessarily the case.

Of course, many iconic corporations have adopted these practices. Some businesses have created entire rooms full of gaming tables, bean-bag chairs and dart boards. There are companies with "nap pods" and free beer and endless snacks all with the thinking that these gimmicks are the key to retaining Millennials.

In reality, some of these efforts are driving Millennials to another job. There are two main reasons. First, consider the message these perks are sending employees. In some cases, Millennials feel that these types of workplace attractions are just a scheme devised to keep them at work longer. Millennials do not even want to be at the office past three in the afternoon, let alone stay past five or six! Some Millennials feel that these are ploys to keep them chained to their cubicle or locked in the confines of Corporate America.

Office Perks or Millennial Traps

The second major issues, larger than the first, is that Millennials feel entrapped by these games. If it was totally socially acceptable, what person would not want to take breaks at work with a round of ping pong? To the Millennial generation, this mid-day break is acceptable. They are typically completing work at a faster pace than some of their older coworkers. As a result, they would prefer to do something rather than sit at their desk and do nothing. So, they pick up a paddle and start volleying with a buddy.

All of a sudden, from around the corner comes their boss yelling at them to get back to work. Or even worse, the passive aggressive boss that cracks the ping pong balls or steals the paddles but will never mention their frustration with the activities. Millennials often feel entrapped. The most important takeaway is not to get rid of some of these extracurricular opportunities. Instead, if a Millennial is away from their cubicle all day sitting in a bean bag chair in the corner, do not judge them. This is a space you have created to be used, so let them use it. Never make a Millennial feel inferior for using perks provided to them by the company.

The best way to manage some of these activities is set boundaries. Remember, Millennials love clear boundaries and they are generally good at playing by the rules. If you have alcohol in your office, you probably do not want your team members day drinking. Set a time of day that your company deems is appropriate for them to pour themselves their favorite beer. If you have gaming consoles or foosball and ping pong, put parameters around it. Either have designated times to play or give them certain milestones in their work they must achieve before blowing off some steam.

Millennials want to please their managers. They do not always do a great job of showing it, but at the core, this is their desire. They want to make you proud of them. They want to hear job well done. They want a trophy. The free games and food also come across as giant distractions to what Millennials really want: to crush their career goals, be a part of something larger than life, and feel engaged while at work.

Millennials are not too concerned about how their workplace looks or the benefits package the company offers. Instead, they are more worried about how it *feels*. Millennials talk about feelings all the time.

Millennials Prefer Warm and Fuzzies over Games

At the end of the day, all they want from a workplace is to feel loved and appreciated. Yes, that means you will have to spend more time thanking them for the small things they do well. Instead of resorting to creating a billiards hall, consider initiatives that will recognize a Millennial's hard work.

Millennials also want to work someplace fun with great people. Millennials thrive on experiences. They want jobs and workplaces that are engaging. So, sometimes this does mean gaming consoles, bean bag chair lounges and movie theaters. But leaders in companies need to think long and hard about why they want to implement these fun items.

More than seventy percent of Millennials want the people they work with to function as a second family. A large part of creating high morale in the office means creating opportunities for meaningful connections between coworkers. As many as ninety percent of Millennials say they wish they worked in an office that was more social. Instead of creating stations where people get distracted from their work, companies should start considering ways to create collaborative work environments and situations where cross-functional team members can interact.

For a Millennial, it is easy to leave a workplace with a ping pong table but is exceedingly difficult for them to part ways with a company where they feel instrumental and connected.

Workplaces that have disconnected employees have been linked to higher rate of absenteeism — nearly forty percent higher. Not only do disconnected team members show up to work less, they also are less present mentally when they are physically at the office. In fact, studies show that there are fifty percent higher rates of bodily accidents and sixty percent higher rates of avoidable mistakes in companies with employees that feel disconnected.

Culture Beats Benefits

Millennials look for jobs with companies that have a strong culture and aligns with their personal values and lifestyle. Their biggest concern is whether or not a job will be worthwhile and will motivate them beyond a paycheck.

Ultimately, Millennials are driven by something that impacts the world around them for the greater good. They prioritize purpose over paycheck. A 2016 Gallup poll revealed that seventy-one percent of Millennials are not engaged at work and its mission. If Millennials are zipping around on hover boards but not connecting with team members or furthering the mission and vision of the company, they will quickly burn out. In fact, sixty percent of Millennials that feel even slightly isolated or disconnected are open to new job opportunities.

Putting proof of your company culture on your website or social media profiles is not enough for a Millennial. If they show up on day one of the job and see signs that the culture does not align, they will start planning their exit strategy. Ping pong tournaments do not equate to company culture. Culture is about the people. To evoke change, you need to influence company culture, not rewrite a company policy.

Millennials are big proponents of company culture. Their first days as new team members are the most important. A great way to onboard a Millennial, and really all team members, is infusing them with your culture. Use their first few days on the job to show them what working at your company is like. Many businesses make the mistake of skipping the onboarding process because they are in desperate need of help. Training is vital for Millennials, so plan accordingly. Millennials need to have a clear path to success. If this is not outlined from the beginning, trying to reel a member of this generation back in is an arduous task.

Research shows that Millennials value, and are most-likely to stick with, companies that have diverse management and leadership, along with flexible work environments. Being global citizens, Millennials are wary of executive teams that all look the same and have the same pedigree. While varying genders and ethnicities are important, Millennials also value competency and character.

The Millennial generation has more individuals that identify as multiracial than any other generation. So, race and ethnicity is an important factor. But it is not the only aspect of diversity that Millennials crave. They also value varying backgrounds and ages. They value an individual's story and how they achieved a seat around the table. If your company does not have diverse leadership, clients, founders, stakeholders... Millennials are not likely to stick around.

Millennials want Interpersonal Relationships

One of the changes in approaches to education during the decades when Millennials were in school was an increased emphasis on teamwork and group projects. From elementary school through college, it was extremely common for members of this generation to be asked to accomplish tasks as part of a team. Not only that, as we have seen, Millennials were often over programmed with extracurriculars, many of which involved team sports or activities.

By structuring your staff in a way that relies on everyone working together with defined roles, you will be able to take advantage of this extensive background in teamwork. For many members of this generational cohort, being a team player is a strength for some of your younger employees. Millennials have strong loyalty to their coworkers, so highlight any opportunities for them to work in teams and put effort towards a common goal.

That said, the comradery that this generation has can sometimes lend itself to a toxic workplace. Sometimes Millennials can get too chummy and begin to grumble about the higher ups in the organization. Unfortunately, this is a common occurrence. The good news is the negative gossip channels are fairly easy to combat.

Most of this underground chatter stems from coworkers banding together over things they dislike about their manager or their organizations. Instead of trying to squash the chatter, an effective leader will help guide the feedback. To overcome the whispers, organizational leadership should be open to listening to team members and be approachable as we talked about several chapters ago. If leadership is approachable, which is different than being always available, than much of this underground chatter can be curbed before it gets out of hand. Lean into the strength of teamwork that Millennials innate have and guide them to be collaborative not just with one another, but with the organization as a whole. Encouraging cross-functional communication and engagement while making organizational leadership accessible will help to minimize silos and maximize trust throughout the organization.

The first day of a Millennial's work might be the most important day of their entire career with your company. Historically, the average human would make a judgments decision in about eleven seconds. Millennials make judgments in about one hundred milliseconds. To put that into perspective, the average time it takes to blink is about four hundred milliseconds. This means Millennials are making judgments approximately four times faster than it takes for them to blink. Again, social media is to blame – scrolling through countless pictures, Millennials are trained to make a snap judgement to like or pass over a photo.

When you hire someone and they are new to the job, it is absolutely critical to make sure that your organization has created an incredible experience for the new hire. That new team member should feel instantly engaged. They should feel like they are appreciated, their role is valued and that they can make a difference.

On day one, that new hire is going to make an instant judgment based on how they are treated, who they meet, what their potential is, what the environment is like, and what the company culture is like. If an organization does not put time and energy into that first day, they may as well have thrown away the whole interview process and everything else in between. Trying to change a Millennial's perspective after they have already set a judgment is very slim.

Millennials want to be connected to their professional role and its worldly impact. They are looking for a job that challenges them, fulfills them, engages them, and allows them to explore ideas and concepts that make a difference. Creating tasks forces that can provide quick breaks in the work week is a great way to engage Millennials on a global level. Having senior leadership take Millennials out for breakfast or lunch can also establish rapport and instill culture far more than ping pong.

Continuing Education keeps Millennials Continually Engaged

If you want to retain your Millennial team members, start with offering some professional development opportunities, as that is the most coveted work benefit to this generational cohort. Does your company offer leadership courses for Millennials? This is a great way to allow Millennials to choose to get involved and better themselves. Another great aspect to offering leadership, management or skills courses is that an organization now has a sign-up roster of engaged team members that are looking to grow. Leadership should descend on these individuals and coach or mentor them. They show great potential and commitment to an organization.

It is true that Millennials get bored if they do not have enough work. On the flip side, if they have a full schedule, they will complain they are too busy. So, how do you combat this? Companies need to equip Millennials with opportunities to prove that they are trustworthy. The majority of Millennials have been babied their whole lives and have been handled with kid gloves. They are longing for affirmation as independent, trustworthy and responsible adults.

A great way to give a Millennial the independence they long for while providing an avenue to earn trust is a flexible work schedule. Too many companies are scared to allow team members to come and go. However, what a company really wants is productivity and engagement. By setting clear expectations about when a team member should be engaged and available as well as what work must be accomplished will establish trust. You will be amazed at how much work Millennials can produce if they have the opportunity to leave early. Not all jobs lend themselves to flex time. Jobs such as customer support, inside sales, and manufacturing jobs, are a bit more challenging to do remotely. Implementing an environment, for the roles where it is possible, that empowers Millennials with flexibility will produce happier and faster working team members. You may also find that the workload is not nearly enough to keep your team busy. If they are completing their tasks and leaving early, you may be able to make up some efficiencies in your organization.

Let your team have some autonomy — skip the micromanaging — which will make them feel a little more free, and they will return the favor by producing better work. Find ways to celebrate in shared achievement, whether through collaborations or offering stock options in the company as a benefit.

So, do not run out and buy a ping pong table. Instead, focus on helping your Millennial employees win in other, career-focused ways.

TRUTH: Millennials would rather go home to enjoy snacks or meet up with their friends to play ping pong than do it at the office. This group is only interested in reaching their career goals and doing so at a company that contributes to the greater good and engages them along the way.

MYTH 7: Millennials Are In An Exclusive Relationship With Technology

Millennials are known for being the first generation of digital natives. They simply do not know life without a computer in some form. Because of this, there is an assumption that many employers and authority figures make about Millennials: that they are addicted to technology.

This assumption hurts this generation more than it helps them. First of all, at the time of this book, the first true Millennials are turning forty. The older portion of the Millennial generation did not grow up with Microsoft Excel, they learned that in their first job. Even the younger Millennials born in the 1990s may not have the skills that many assume they possess. Many times, Millennials of all ages are tossed into jobs that require specific technological skills that they may not have learned. As many as thirty-two percent of Millennials do not have work-related computer skills, such as those associated with Microsoft Word, Excel or other software programs. Millennials still need trained on many enterprise systems like Oracle, Salesforce, Hubspot and others. As a generally proud generation, Millennials are unlikely to ask for help, especially when it comes to technology. They know they are often viewed as experts. Be sure to equip all team members with the necessary tools and resources to learn the technology that your organization uses.

The second large misnomer about Millennials and technology is thinking that electronic communication is the only way a Millennial can collaborate, talk and learn. Millennials long for social interactions and face-to-face communication. It is especially powerful when leadership interfaces with a Millennial in person. It establishes trust and builds rapport. On the other hand, if digital communication is used and a Millennial does not receive a response to an email for a day or two, they can start to feel underappreciated and undervalued. Electronic communication is a double-edged sword.

Communication is very important to Millennials. All forms of communicating help Millennials to feel connected, not just virtual communication.

Millennials want to be Taught

Another common misconception among leaders in companies is the fact that Millennial generation can only learn from technology. Corporations are spending countless dollars on virtual learning management systems. This is a great advancement for companies, but it is not an end all be all. Millennials, just like every other generation, have different learning styles. Some are auditory learners, others visual and still other hands-on learners. Providing online continuing education is a great way to keep employees engaged. However, providing offline learning and fostering an environment of collaboration is a way to anchor Millennials in a team environment creating a stickiness factor.

In general, Millennials do learn differently in that they require more specialized, multimedia teaching strategies. The later-born Millennials never saw transparencies, chalkboards or slide projectors. Instead, they were in classrooms with video projectors and white boards. Lucky them, they did not have to bang out chalky erasers behind the school as a punishment.

Even though this generation grew up with access to computers, smartphones and the internet throughout their education, they still long for traditional teaching. They love learning. With quick access to knowledge, Millennials are always looking up facts and trying to be as educated as possible.

Consider using a hybrid of traditional and e-learning methodologies. A diverse set of learning strategies for your company will engage Millennials and older generations alike. Further, a key factor of learning for Millennials is multi-generational teaching environments. Many of the educators online on platforms such as YouTube are younger. While Millennials enjoy learning a quick how-to online, they love interacting with mentors and coaches from more mature generations that can impart wisdom. Creating a multi-generational learning environment will help Millennials feel connected to your organization as a whole.

Though Millennials do enjoy traditional corporate education along with e-learning, they do have some different needs. With a shorter attention span, getting your Millennials to sit through long lectures is not going to do the trick. When performing a training session, be sure to change the formats to maintain interest and appeal to different learners in the group. Some people prefer audio or visual lessons, while others may need hands-on activities. Go at it with the approach of having fewer lectures and more collaborative, group-based projects.

Steve Jobs, when doing an Apple product unveiling, would often format the big reveal in short chunks. Every seven to ten minutes, he would change up the speaker, play a video, or conduct a product demo. This change in rhythm keeps audiences engaged.

When teaching corporation specific materials, it is important to connect the lessons to the context of your office. Continually point back to corporate values. Again, Millennials love learning and career development, they love interactions with co-workers and leadership, and finally, they love working towards the bigger picture. If you can continually point your ongoing training back to your core values, you will be able to engage a Millennial at an emotional level, not just an intellectual one.

Further, using concrete examples that relate to your organization will help your team members apply what they have learned to specific situations they may face while on the job. Another important method is to explain the rationale behind the lesson. Remember, that Baby Boomers take everything at face value — if you say it is true, they will believe it. Millennials need a little bit more convincing. They do not give respect just because they are *supposed* to, and they are not going to do something just because you *said* so.

A relaxed learning environment also benefits the Millennials on your team. As a rule this group does not like to be pressured to do things that seem meaningless or mundane. Instead, they are always seeking more freedom to complete tasks and ways to express their creativity. This generation is also interested in building relationships. If there is a way to combine learning with networking, use that as an opportunity to engage Millennials.

Millennials long for Mentors

Millennials are dependent on using the internet for their source of knowledge and learning. Chances are, they do not feel comfortable going to a manager for advice. They are afraid of looking inferior or incompetent. The reality is, Millennial employees want to learn from their coworkers and mentors. They just do not know where to start. Part of it is pride and part of it is a fear of coming across like they cannot do the job at hand.

Often, if the lines of communication for mentorship is not opened, Millennials turn to the internet for advice. I am sure you have used Google to search for something online. Perhaps you have seen the suggested search phrases that come up as you start typing. For a fun experiment, go to Google and start typing "How do I" or "How do you." Look at some of the search suggestions!

Have you ever wondered, "Who in the world would search for *that*?" It was likely a Millennial. They search for things other generations asked their friends or family members for.

Yes, Millennials are the first generation to grow up with the internet as an everyday part of their lives. They are the first to embrace and take advantage of technology that connects people electronically. This experience and knowledge can help expand communication both internally and externally for your firm. Do not mistake an affinity for technology with knowing everything that has to do with computers.

This generation could also use help with other professional skills, too. As many as fifty-six percent of Millennials are not equipped with soft skills such as communication, listening, patience, leadership and relationship building. Often, Millennials are promoted — or they think they should be promoted —

before they have a handle on these important skill sets. Providing them the opportunities to learn these things as a way to earn a promotion is certainly a way to retain Millennials.

Take all of this as a way to be a mentor to your Millennial employees by providing them regular feedback (as much as weekly), always keep the communication lines open, and provide them with new challenges that will help them learn skills in non-traditional ways.

Of course, no manager has time to walk their employees through learning every lesson. Figure out ways to engage other company leadership. Additionally, it is so important to create a culture of autonomous learning. Companies should equip team members with both structured and unstructured, digital and in-person learning opportunities. Some of the best learning a team can have is in-person an unstructured. This can create a culture of collaboration, acceptance and growth. Each of these are something Millennials long for in a job.

Communicating Tasks

It is important to note that Millennials are often yes-men, and they will say yes to anything that's in front of them, which usually results in them feeling overwhelmed. If a Millennial is given a lot of tasks without a lot of direction, they struggle to understand what to do and how to prioritize it.

This goes back to how Millennials' entire lives have been scheduled. They are not used to being able to prioritize on their own, so Millennials often have a difficult time distinguishing between what is important and what is urgent. Similarly, they have trouble deciphering between a recommendation and a requirement.

A large part in managing Millennials is giving them clear directions, allowing them the ability to have creativity, but also showing them the importance of managing their time and clearly indicating what's important and what can wait. Millennials are more focused on the end-result, and sometimes they could use some tips on how to get there in the best way possible.

Millennials are hard workers who get results, but to connect with them and retain them, you might have to be willing to live with a more flexible schedule and unique learning opportunities.

Millennial's arrival in the workforce is a challenge, but also an opportunity. Managers from previous generations stand to learn more about the world we live in and to make better decisions accordingly. Millennials are here to stay. Let's make the most of it.

TRUTH: Millennials are comfortable using computers, but many of them lack specific software skills needed on the job. Just like any other generation, individuals in this one have different learning preferences and need guidance as they work through their career path. Despite assumptions, this generation could use mentoring to learn a variety of skills they have yet to discover.

Conclusion

At the end of the day, the Millennial generation is like every preceding generation – unique. Each one of us is characterized by our backgrounds. Where, when and how we were raised each play a foundational role in transforming us into the adults that we ultimate become.

When it comes to leadership, the best leaders are those that are introspective enough to understand their own strengths and weaknesses while being intuitive enough to tailor communication towards a team member's strengths and weaknesses.

Surveying the generations past, present and future provide a framework through which one can gauge attitudes and perspectives. Each generation values various work ethics and attitudes. Views of authority, money, family and the world shift and morph overtime. Media is a major influencer in each generation as is innovation. Developments and changes cause children to be raised in a different way than their parents. This causes the generational divide.

While this book was intended to provide context towards leading and managing members of various generations, it will not solve each and every problem. Instead, the purpose of this book was to equip you with the knowledge you need to better tailor the way in which you lead your team and organization.

The myths are just a few of the many knocks against Millennials that I have heard over the years. Though I have attempted to debunk and deconstruct a number of the labels, there are still countless scenarios that were not covered. The truth is, some of the myths may not be myths in your organization. There are lazy, disrespectful, anti-social and entitled Millennials. Many of those attributes could be assigned to members of other generations as well.

The most important thing to walk away with after you close this book is to remember, leadership is a two-way street. The most influential leaders do not remain stagnant. They are not set in their ways. Instead, they adapt, learn and grow. Many people ask me how to change Millennials. In reality, you cannot change someone else until you are willing to embrace change yourself. Often, you will have to change some of your methods and tactics to reach the rising generation. This does not mean, however, that you should do all the heavy lifting. What it does mean is that you should be willing to pivot at times and coach when needed to help set the next generation up for optimal success.

Having arrived at this point, you have now full received the cypher that you will need to crack the millennial code.

Made in the USA
Monee, IL
11 February 2023

27494632R00072